MW01221863

The Shamanic Journey

of *Living as Soul*

WINGED WOLF

(Heather Hughes-Calero)

Cover Illustration by Diane Forney

Higher Consciousness Books
1994

Cover Illustration by Diane Forney
Cover Design by Nan Perrott

Winged Wolf, Soul Vision, The Eagle Tribe and
The Tribe of Eagles are registered trade names.

Higher Consciousness Books
Division of Coastline Publishing Company
Post Office Box 1806, Sedona, Arizona 86339
Phone/Fax (602) 634-7728

Printed in the United States of America

Library of Congress Catalog No.: 94-084298
ISBN: 0-932927-11-4

WITH APPRECIATION

To my mother Vi Maticic, who typed a portion of this book prior to her illness. To Janie Dick and Robin Littlefield, who accepted the task of proofreading the entire text on very short notice. To Ellouese Upton for her very valuable companion energy.

Also to ...
>
Mary Lee
Sharon Huxford
Walter Huxford
Suzanne Williams
Pat Natale

for compiling the quotations used in this book, which
I LOVINGLY DEDICATE TO ALL OF MY APPRENTICES.

CONTENTS

Part 1

Part 2

Part 3

Part 4

THE DELICATE SONG OF GRASS GROWING 104

"A quiet mind makes it
possible to double,
to walk through the
dimensions of time and space,
to be omnipresent.
We are not talking about
out-of-the-body
experiences, but, rather,
stepping from one
reality into another, using
matter as a hinge."

Winged Wolf

NOT A SEASON FOR DANDELION LEAVES

In the early morning of February 24th, the postman knocked at my door with a package from my shaman teacher Alana Spirit Changer. There was no mystery to it, like there was the first time, which I wrote about in CIRCLE OF POWER. On this occasion, as well, however, Alana was presenting me the eagle stick she had given me a few years ago. I had returned my stick to her early last December as a way of telling her that I needed her to stay in the world to assist me, after she had announced that she was going to translate (die). This time the stick signaled me to her side.

There was a light in her cave and it felt warm even though it was only February in Colorado. Alana was sitting up on her sleeping rug, waiting for me. Her eyes met mine as I presented myself to her, and I was consumed by the warm glow of her love. She didn't appear sick. She seemed healthy and vital and her face was radiant. As I gazed at her, I realized that it was her light that filled the room; that her powerful life force produced the light, and that she was the light itself.

"Hello, my daughter," she said sweetly.

"Hello, mother of Soul," I answered.

There was a long pause before she said, "It is nearly time for me to leave you."

Gazing at her powerful, but beautiful countenance, I silently asked why, and I told her that now, more than ever, I needed her.

Alana smiled. "You need me because you love me," she said.

It was true. I loved her for countless, nameless reasons, loving her as I loved myself and the purpose and vitality she had opened up in my life. She was now so much more to me than my teacher. The shaman in her was the God-part that lived in me.

In the long unspeaking silence, I argued that I not only loved her, but that, without her, I felt only half of myself. How could I possibly succeed at my work without her at my side?

She quickly answered my thought. "You will fulfill the work you have chosen to do." She paused, a glimmer of excitement filled her eyes and then faded again. "For a time, you may feel alone, until you realize why I am going." Looking into her eyes as she spoke, I saw a reflection of myself with her, as one. The scene prompted me to recall our first meeting years ago, when as we drove together to the Colorado ranch my Uncle Farley had left me in his Will, as told in WOMAN BETWEEN THE WIND. Watching me detect the scene depicted in her eyes, she nodded. "The message in the scene originated in its production," she said softly.

I knew that Alana referred to the bond of energy between us and that, while we had traveled a great distance together spiritually, our initial unification was the same then and now. For a long while I remained motionless looking at her. She was not old, although not young either. The long dark hair hanging loose around her shoulders reminded me of a mane on one of the wild horses she had nurtured in the hollow of the mountains outside her cave. They would miss her. Her leaving would be like the breath being sucked out of their lives, as well. "Please stay another year," I murmured.

"Heather, can you hear me?" Alana whispered.

She spoke so softly that I quickly moved closer to hear what she would say.

"Would you go and find me some dandelion leaves?"

Startled, I moved back and stared at her. It was February in Colorado, not a season for dandelion leaves.

"Please," the medicine woman whispered sweetly. I leaned closer to hear the rest of her words. "They could effect a healing."

There were dandelion plants growing on the roadside at the base of my mailbox in Cottonwood, Arizona where I lived. I was carefully uprooting some of the young plants sprouting there, when the mail truck drove up.

"Good morning," the driver called out. It was a different delivery person than the one who had delivered the box with my eagle stick earlier. "Good morning," I answered back.

"See you're pulling spring weeds before they multiply," the postperson said.

"Dandelion is also good for the digestion," I answered, rising to take the mail from him.

"That so?" He handed me a stack of letters. "Do all the people who write to you know about dandelions?"

"Some do," I answered, taking the mail from him and putting it on the ground while I carefully extracted a root from the earth. The mail truck drove off. When I had gathered a few of the plants growing there, I picked up my mail from the ground and returned to Alana's cave. I found her preparing hot water for tea. I handed her the dandelion plants and watched as she cleaned the dirt off the roots and placed the entire plants into the boiled water and left them to steep. "Looks like you received many letters today," she commented, observing the stack of letters I held in my hand.

"Yes," I answered, "from my apprentices."

"Let's look at them," Alana said.

We sat down on her sleeping rug. I thumbed through the envelopes, stopped at one from an apprentice who frequently had many questions. I told her this about the apprentice and remarked that they were usually interesting questions, and that I felt the individual to have the makings of a shaman.

"Let's open it up," Alana said eagerly.

Dear Winged Wolf:

Would you please tell me more about shaman teachers and what traits a teacher would like in an apprentice?

Alana touched my hand, stopping me from reading on. "What would you say to her?" she asked.

I explained that I had been writing a book titled THE SHAMANIC JOURNEY OF LIVING AS SOUL, and that it was filled with information on this subject and others. "In fact," I said, "I wrote an article on "Choosing a Shaman Teacher."

"Read it to me," Alana said.

"Now?"

"There is no other time."

We both laughed. Alana had made a pun. Not only was there no other time for her, because her life was coming to an end; but, since all life ONLY existed in the present moment, there was no other time.

I left Alana and quickly entered my home-office, turned the computer on to access the files on my new book. Once accessed, I printed them out on paper and with an air of excitement took them to Alana in her cave.

"It means so much to me to share my work with you," I said. "Who else can I share moments like this with?" I knew my voice was filling with emotion but I could not bear to have her leave me.

"Read me about 'Choosing a Shaman Teacher,'" she said.

I got a grip on myself and thumbed through the pages until I came to the topic. Then I read to Alana:

HOW TO CHOOSE A SHAMAN TEACHER

You can look and look and look for a shaman teacher and never find one. This is because a shaman teacher usually finds you. If they are a publicly visible teacher, say a writer, they may have a striking influence on you while you are reading their book. And most likely, you came in contact with their book in an unusual way. Maybe it fell off the shelf at your local bookstore and struck you in the head.

But then, your shaman teacher may not be a writer at all. He or she may be a horse-back-riding instructor. You may meet and study horsemanship with them, only to learn that something much greater is occurring in your education. My apprentices come from all walks of life. Some are doctors, some lawyers, some administrative personnel, athletics, artists, you name it. Some day many of these people will be shaman, and many will teach. They may teach through their profession, whatever it may be. How will you know who they are?

Most likely, you'll have a striking familiarity, a feeling that you have a connection to the shaman who will teach you. You will simply know "This is it!" when you meet your shaman teacher. You will feel

drawn to them, curious about them, accompanied
with a feeling reminiscent of being attracted to them,
as one does before falling in love. The feelings may, for
a time, confuse you and beguile you, but not for long.
As you interact with this person, there is a recognition
that they are someone different than anyone you have
ever met; that they have an incredible presence about
them; a powerful life force; a clarity of mind and, in
talking to them, you sense that they know everything
about you, even though you have only met.

"A shaman is always a medicine woman or medicine man, but a medicine woman or medicine man is not always a shaman. In addition to being a healer, a shaman is omniscient and omnipresent in his or her abilities."

Circle of Power
Page 40

"Shaman have a way of falling into knowledge belts."

Circle of Power
Page 121

"A medicine woman is not limited by viewpoint. A medicine woman is one who shape shifts to become what her student needs her to be, and yet she has her own individual nature, which designates her power medicine."

Flight of Winged Wolf
Page 48

"A medicine woman's acts are always aware. Awareness of her nature and her links with others provide her with the power that she needs to do her work."

Circle of Power
Page 38/39

"I told you to stop believing in things. When you believe in things, you shut off the possibility of making the unknown known. A shaman never has her doors closed."

Circle of Power
Page 13

"The way of a medicine woman is to accept responsibility for everything that happens in her life. By your innermost being, you control the way you are accepted or rejected by the environment."

Circle of Power
Page 14

I paused. Alana looked at me in a way that told me to go on. I continued reading.

USING A SHAMAN TEACHER

When you have earned your place in the sun, meaning when life grants you a shaman teacher, give yourself to her/him. That doesn't mean you give all of your possessions to the teacher. On the contrary, your teacher won't be interested in your possessions, except that she will be grateful that you have them. She will be grateful, because the spiritual life provides abundance in all areas of one's life. The fact that you have accumulated possessions and live abundantly, at least materially, is encouraging to the teacher who has to otherwise consider your financial problems along with everything else.

Giving yourself to a teacher means to let go of your ideas of things, your attitudes and your opinions and replace them with viewpoints your teacher exhibits for you. In this way you will be given a broader and freer perspective of life.

It also means to submit to the teacher, without grabbing for what the teacher teaches, and without resisting it either. The apprentices that grab at knowledge are looking for instant enlightenment. They want to know what the teacher knows now and add and compare it to what they "think" they already know. Seekers of this sort will never reach spiritual heights, because they are not willing to live what they learn. They are merely collectors. Resistant apprentices are also unwilling to live what they learn because they are afraid of the unknown and therefore, afraid to trust the teacher. The very fact that they are resistant means that they are pulling and pushing at the same time. Usually, this latter type of apprentice can be helped, but the teacher will have to be smart enough to trick him into "letting go." My teacher was very smart, so smart that she turned her back on me and did not speak to me for over a year. What this did to me was force my attention onto her. To this day, my life is a song of gratitude and praise. It was a drastic measure for my teacher, but I was an apprentice who had to be treated with drastic measures.

It used to be that I felt too good to sleep on her floor, now I know I wasn't good enough. If ever I become a teacher as great as she, it will be because of the way she treated me, which infused her shaman qualities into me by my longings for her. Can you see the law of opposites at work here? It is a painful way to learn. I do not recommend it to anyone. The proper way to use a teacher is easy. Be respectful. Do as you are told. Trust. Relax. Enjoy the journey.

"It is important to remember three things. One, is that nothing matters. Two is that you don't have to understand anything; and three, that there is no competition between us."

Woman Between the Wind
Page 109

"I do nothing. It's chemistry, the blending of one spirit with another spirit that effects change, and what happens is not for me to say. Whatever change there is comes from what is ready to become. Spirit is the essence of a person, but not a person's Soul."

Woman Between the Wind
Page 37

"It's good to have uncertainties. One cannot progress without a creative imagination."

Woman Between the Wind
Page 142

"Holes are areas of infection in one's life. It is a shaman's role to clean out the infection and to fill the holes."

Woman Between the Wind
Page 127

"Your medicine wheel vision merely opens the door to a life experience. It is the life experience that follows that is the true teacher. I can only offer you images and direction, but life will teach you in a way you will never forget."

Woman Between the Wind
Page 71

"There are two types of students. One is an alive student who simply approaches the teacher with 'Here I am!' The alive student has no preconceived concepts or opinions in the face of her teacher's knowledge. The other student is a dead student, one who is too full to receive from the teacher. The dead student always tries to compare what she thinks she knows with what the teacher says, picking at the gifts that are given."

Woman Between the Wind
Page 149

"If you poke someone and there is no response, you can't put something into them. A teacher pokes a student until that student lets go of her personal history, meaning she eliminates her rigid attitudes and aberrations."

Flight of Winged Wolf
Page 137

"A shaman doesn't change things in people, a shaman fixes things."

Flight of Winged Wolf
Page 20

"Be yourself in every way that you can. It is the impeccable way of medicine women and men."

Flight of Winged Wolf
Page 55

"A teacher empowers her apprentice, which is why a teacher is necessary."

Circle of Power
Page 39

I paused again. This time Alana lightly touched my arm. "Your apprentices have it easier than you did."

I gazed into her eyes. By her words, she meant that my relationship with her had been all guess-work on my part. My apprentices had the benefit of written, as well as personal communication with me. Learning something always made it easier if there was material to read while discovering one's lessons.

"It is what makes it possible for you to have many apprentices. If I had had more than you, Winged Wolf, I would have been murdered."

We laughed, but I knew what she said was true. Even as her only apprentice, I often threw my anger at her, which was destructive to her body. At times it made her ill, because she did not reflect my anger back at me. Instead, to protect me, she allowed it to pass through her body to transmute it.

"Go on with your book," Alana prodded.

BECOMING A SHAMAN TEACHER

If you desire to become a shaman teacher, please listen carefully.

You will become a shaman teacher when you are ready. Please, please don't try to become a shaman teacher without first apprenticing with a shaman who apprenticed and became shaman. The word shaman indicates a state of consciousness and powers aligned with that state of consciousness. If you cannot be the real thing, forget it. Right now, the world is full of people, and this applies to some Native

American people, as well, calling themselves shaman simply to get on the bandwagon.

There is great responsibility to BEing shaman. First of all, it can't be pretended. When you meet someone who is really shaman you will know the difference. Shaman is a consciousness a person wears. One who is shaman lives as Soul, with impeccable intent, and possesses the demeanor of one who stands alone. The power of one who lives as shaman can be explained simply as one who has the freedom to live omnipresently, inside and outside the worlds of time and space.

"We are all students. It is the most dedicated of all students who become the best teachers. The best teachers are the ones who are always learning. People who are not learning should not teach."

Circle of Power
Page 9

"I am my teachers, not in personality or expression, but I am the power my teachers possessed, therefore, I, too, am possessed."

Circle of Power
Page 122

Alana had been listening with her eyes closed and she now opened them. "Some people will not like what you say, but they will know that what you are saying is true, Heather."

Experience had taught me this and I said nothing in reply.

"Read me more."

I turned the pages until I came to a heading on REALITY.

"Yes, read me what you have written," Alana said.

I leaned back against the rock wall and propped the papers on my knees, then began reading again.

REALITY

Reality is really quite different than what most people imagine it to be. Most people look at reality as time and space, as well as agreed upon sequences of events that take place within time and space. To these people, reality means you are seeing the world the same as I do, or vice versa, me seeing it the same as they are. Viewing life in this way is an agreed upon sociological mindset. Everyone agrees, so that's the way it is.

The sociological mindset evolves, according to the mind expansiveness of the times. Whatever is being mentally invented now, becomes tomorrow's reality. And, much of what was mentally invented in the past yields to the change in ideas. This is why religions are making dramatic changes. The mental inventions of so-called religious "supernatural mysteries" - heaven,

24

hell and purgatory - no longer convince the imaginations of most modern people. Now they are concerned with "right thinking" to make life more enjoyable and ideas of after-life more palatable.

The Spiritual Warrior, the individual who lives at the Third Eye, located in the center of her forehead, maintains a keen overview of the mass consciousness reality and can freely pick and choose her lifestyle within it, without getting caught up in it. This individual's reality is not limited by time and space, nor by the mass consciousness mental inventions that confine life within this realm. The Spiritual Warrior lives only by the single rule of a reality that says, "With total responsibility comes total freedom." Thus, the person who lives as Soul, enjoys abundance, freedom and happiness in the world without being bogged down by influences.

What is reality?
Reality is the absence of limitation.

"The environment I see and relate to is a symbol of my consciousness. By taking appearances as illustrations means I know all appearances are illusionary."

Woman Between the Wind
Page 15

"There are two ends to the stick. One is thought, mind, and the other is consciousness or Soul."

Flight of Winged Wolf
Page 63

"The balance point is where you can weigh both sides of a situation or get a detached view of going one way or the other. From this point you will see that the mountain is no greater than the valley....no good end of the stick and no bad end."

Flight of Winged Wolf
Page 63

"...the image you carry in mind and consciousness predicts the outcome of an energy match."

Flight of Winged Wolf
Page 64

"People's realities are quite different from each other, much more so than you realize."

Woman Between the Wind
Page 56

"The only common reality that exists is the place. The nature of the place and what it looks like varies from person to person, except those parts about which a common agreement has been made."

Woman Between the Wind
Page 57

"A burning desire to go in a
particular direction means that
you are sitting in your seat
of power and wanting to
give it up."

Flight of Winged Wolf
Page 66

THE CYCLE OF LIFE

Basically, there are three stages to the cycle of life. The first takes place from birth to puberty. In this first stage of life, the individual looks out at the world, filled with wonder and awe, feeling somewhat diminished by the seemingly greatness of people and events. At puberty, there is a change. Whereas, up until the age of twelve, when the individual is the person his peers say he is, there is a growing awareness of one's place within the environment and a genuine interest in the nature of one's self. This turns the attention inward, internalizing the world and one's experience in it. For the next twenty years or so, the individual struggles to understand one's self and one's relationship with others. During this time there is a desire to be accepted by peers, and to be filled with the presence of one special other. This looking in at one's self is a time of emotional experience. Like the up and down movement of a see-saw, there is great happiness one moment, and discontentedness, even despair the next. For many, this stage of life continues until death. Day in and day out, they ride the see-saw of emotional life, victims of circumstances.

For those few who have a truly bold and adventuresome outlook, who exhibit a determination to inquiry into a greater meaning to life, there appears a teacher to direct their attention to the Third Eye, where they learn to live as Soul in a physical body. At this final stage in the cycle, the individual looks out at the world again, not the same as in infancy, but an enriched version of infancy's gaze. The time spent looking in, staring at one's person in the mirror of self-reflection, now enhances the new looking out. The individual becomes whole, centered as Soul in the body, and the experience is divine - joy and freedom, unlike anything previously encountered.

JOY

Please don't misunderstand the word bliss. It is does not mean that one becomes silly and dysfunctional in life. On the contrary, one who has achieved this state can mingle with the societies of the world, being one with all, while not a part of all. A person living in the true joy state is wise, kind, and loving to those they meet, however, that does not mean that they are not beheld as awesome or even strange. Who is looking at whom? The enlightened person looks at the unenlightened with compassion, while an unenlightened person may see the enlightened one as unusual and fear him. It must be remembered, however, that he/she who perceives another as awesome or strange is simply witnessing a variation from their own definition of normal.

No greater experience is there than the experience of joy. It is the breath of the VOID made manifest in our lives. And what I have to say about Joy is no mere grouping of words. Joy is, in truth, the breath of God. We are not talking about a God that is outside of you, but God that is apart of you.

How is this possible?

You, as Soul are a part of God. When, through

experience, you come to realize this simple fact, the joy that is produced in your life is truly incredible. Its existence within you has nothing to do with the weather conditions, or people's attitudes toward you, but rather, it is wholly existent because of your awareness, and is, therefore, with you always. Hindu religions refer to this state as Samadhi, meaning that through unification with the ONE there is bliss. To be shaman means to live in this state of consciousness.

FREEDOM

To have freedom means that you are ready to assume responsibility for yourself. No longer are you the victim of circumstances. For the individual who is free there is no such thing as luck. Freedom comes to those who know, not only the strong and the weak of themselves, but know themselves as Soul. These are the people who have learned to live at the Third Eye center. They are whole and happy in every way, because as free beings they take charge of themselves.

Freedom means lack of worry or concern of the outcome of an endeavor, because to worry, one would have to give up her feeling of freedom. Consequently, the person who has freedom lives abundantly within the body of God and all things are possible. A truly free person can fly with the eagles, or swim the depths of the sea with dolphins. A truly free person has the power to live without boundaries of time and space, omnipresently.

How does one win freedom?

"By listening to one's true self, the inner voice, and acting in accordance with it. But first one must acknowledge the parts of oneself that blocks freedom, otherwise what we believe to be the inner voice is merely the chattering of our shortcomings speaking to us."

Woman Between the Wind
Page 96/97

"Many people function with a fractured personality because they don't feel they have a right to live as they wish."

Flight of Winged Wolf
Page 55

FEELING

My teacher Alana Spirit Changer used to say to me, that "life was a feeling" and that without feeling there was no life. Feeling, then, is the motivating force that propels one moment into the next. Not only does it move life in a linear forward motion, but feelings provide anchor points through which we can feel moments past. Anchor points are memories kept alive through feeling and without them only the present moment exists, alive by its feeling. This latter position is the seat of power for the enlightened person. With the attention wholeheartedly on the present moment, the feeling of divine love fills one's heart and overflows into life to uplift the whole.

"Winged Wolf," Alana said, touching my arm again, this time as a signal to stop reading. I looked into her eyes. "You have to explain the Third Eye more, otherwise people will never understand what you are trying to tell them."

I explained to her that the next part of the book contained a dialogue I had had with some apprentices.

"Oh, good," she said. "Read it to me."

PART 2

A DIALOGUE WITH APPRENTICES

Winged Wolf: We are going to talk about Soul Vision, or living as Soul in a physical body, and how to recognize and develop that perspective, which comes to us through our Soul faculty of direct perception. This dialogue is going to develop as you develop and you pose questions. We are speaking about you personally, and you as a part of the whole. Do you follow me?

Questioner: You are saying that the perspective of Soul Vision cannot develop without the development of mass acceptance.

Winged Wolf: Exactly. That is to say that there is no development of anything without first placing the attention on an area to be developed. If you want to prove this to yourself, take a look at science, which says that nothing exists without proof. Without confirmation of a thing, the realities derived from it cannot exist because the precept doesn't live in an individual's life. If you don't know about Soul Vision; better yet, if you don't know how to do it, and do it, the perspective of living as Soul means nothing. To you, it wouldn't exist.

Questioner: But not existing to me wouldn't mean that it doesn't exist.

Winged Wolf: You must pay attention to what I said. I said to you it would not exist, meaning, if you were not aware of it, it would have no meaning to you.

Questioner: Isn't Soul Vision something that we all do whether we are aware of it or not?

Winged Wolf: Yes, but one's lack of awareness interferes with one's being able to live it, which is to use it. Without awareness, and I am speaking about conscious awareness via direct perception, you cannot consciously initiate a state of consciousness. Soul Vision is a state of consciousness, rather than what most people think of as a tool. It is not a tool at all. It is a state of consciously living as Soul.

Questioner: How does one do that?

Winged Wolf: Soul Vision itself is brought about through the relaxation of the eyes, having the attention here (taps center of forehead) on the Tisra Til or Third Eye, and moving through life, doing whatever you need to do, in that way. When you move through life with your attention on the Third Eye, the mind is clipped off and there is no mental chatter going on in your head. So, you are free to accomplish whatever you want. There is no conflict! If you have a goal, a target, or something you want to do, the mind is not saying, "Well, you can't do that," or That won't work. Don't you remember, you tried that ten years ago and it didn't work then. Why should it work now?" Or..."Why should it work? So and so said that they tried that and it didn't work for them. You know how really good at it that they are and still they failed. What makes you think you could succeed if they couldn't?"

All of these contrary statements go on inside the mind.

Questioner: Why is that?

Winged Wolf: It is the nature of the mind to be that way. When we start to do something, and somebody says, "That won't work," immediately a button pushes a light inside of our mind and we reflect back to experiences we've had in the past with other situations or something we have heard about in someone else's experiences. The light inside of our mind flashes a warning and we say, "Yes, they are right," or "It may not work," or "It won't work," and we set up blocks. So, what we want to do is eliminate this mind chatter that goes on so that we can go directly to whatever it is that we want to do. If we want to get a cup of tea from the kitchen, there is no conflict that says, "No, you shouldn't have that cup of tea," or "What kind of tea are you going to have," going back and forth in making decisions and this kind of yakity yak that goes on inside of the brain.

Questioner: How can it be avoided? It is normal and natural to have a conversation inside of your head.

Winged Wolf: I am saying to you that it is not natural, although in our society it may be considered normal, because people have forgotten their purpose to live as Soul. When we go directly forward, with our attention on the Third Eye, the brain is alert and functioning, but the conflict, or the opposition, or the outside images, are not coming inside of us to change what it is that we set out to do.

Living as Soul, we are free! Free in a way that we have never before experienced. This is the best part, the freedom. And you know, everybody talks about freedom, but nobody says how to have it. How do we become free?

Questioner: By allowing others to have their freedom.

Winged Wolf: Yes, that is true, but you are mouthing words, thinking of clever things to say, and then saying them. That's not what we're after. I want to really look at this business of living as Soul and how we can do it, and you want to theorize on its effects.

This freedom through living as Soul thing goes back to the beginning of time. The Hindus knew about it once. Today their married women wear a little red dot in the center of their foreheads, indicating they belong to someone. So you see, they have forgotten what the center of the forehead meant. But, way back in the beginning, people knew what it was to keep your attention here (taps forehead) at the Third Eye. People lived it. It was the "normal" way to live, just as it is normal to live in our minds today.

Newborn babies are pure Soul. Gradually, as their attention is drawn to objects, they look at objects, and they start focusing "hard focus" on objects, because people are saying, "Pay attention to this. Pay attention to that." So infants begin to get their focus zeroed in on something, and gradually they forget this relaxed vision (Soul Vision), which is how the magic of life is actually performed, by living as Soul.

Basically, what Soul Vision does, is that by keeping attention on the Third Eye, you can go through life and achieve anything that you want to achieve, without opposition to what you are achieving. You can go right to the top of the ladder in a career field; you can write a novel; you can write any kind of a book; you can become a fine artist, a musician, a doctor or a lawyer - anything at all.

You can balance your checkbook while living as Soul (in Soul Vision). People say, "Oh well, you know, I have to work on my checkbook now. I can't possibly stay as Soul and do my accounting." Or, they say, "My job is so demanding, I can't possibly live as Soul." YES, YOU CAN! And, it makes the task easier. It cuts through all the junk, the confusion in life, because there is none of this yakity yak going on inside of the brain.

Questioner: (Mumbles something about not wanting to be brainless.)

Winged Wolf: That doesn't say that the brain is not a very powerful instrument in this process. As a matter of fact, it is more powerful than it has ever been, because it isn't all cluttered up. It is clear, without conflict, or pro and con arguments going on inside of it. When you are living as Soul, the brain can function without interference. When you start to go and do something, how often are you sidetracked? How often are you pulled this way and that way - somebody gets your attention to do this and gets your attention to do that? In this way it may take months to accomplish something that should be completed in a day or two. You see, when you are not living as Soul, you are never really on target for what you are doing. Oddly enough, when you are in Soul Vision, even though your peripheral senses are relaxed, you are aware and have much greater awareness. You can zero in towards a goal and take care of everything else at the same time.

I have a phenomenal schedule. People have difficulty setting appointments with me, because I really am busy most of the time. I have many things that I have to take care of. But, I can take care of it all, because I live as Soul...about eighty-five percent of the time, not a hundred percent. I don't know of anyone who lives a hundred percent, but maybe you get there. The spiritual journey is always on-going. You never arrive. The idea is that, when you live as Soul, there is ultimate power always at hand - to do whatever it is you want to do.

Now, as questions are coming up in you, I want to dialogue so that we can really give you an idea of what this Soul Vision is, and how it can serve each and every one of you in life, not surface talk. We can use examples. We can get into everyday life and prove how it works. Don't accept my words simply because they make sense, because shaman-ism is a path of DO. It's not a path about talking about DOing. It is DOing. So, let's learn how we can apply Soul Vision to different things that are happening in our individual lives. Does anybody have anything they want to bring up?

Questioner: Well, in my life right now, there are so many things going on. My husband is thinking about going back to Washington to live, to complete what he needs to do there and to get away from the energy of our present life. He is finding it very difficult to live in this environment, and he is not able to find a job.

Winged Wolf: Is there a question here? How are you going to relate what you are saying to Soul Vision?

Questioner: To Soul Vision? Okay. I have found myself getting in the way, saying to myself, "I can't let him go," or "If he goes what is going to happen to me. I have never been alone in my *life. How is all this going to"....(hesitates) and it just about drives me crazy.*

I wanted to hold onto my husband, and then I realized that by getting into Soul Vision, and the feeling I could survive. By letting my husband go, I was giving him a way of finding out who he was. I can find out who I really am, and knowing that I could take care of myself, I shut off all of the "You can'ts" and "You never."

Winged Wolf: It's frightening to go through major changes in life, especially when you have an image of a person who is anchored to you and suddenly, you are faced with letting go of that anchor.

Questioner: Yes, and now living in Soul Vision I realize that there was a point in time when I was in love with him differently - with claws in, manipulating and controlling. I understand that now, and now, I truly love him. And I'm grateful to him for the time in life we had together.

Winged Wolf: And you can let him be.

Questioner: And I can let him be, and it doesn't hurt.

Winged Wolf: Isn't that wonderful!

Questioner: And I know a few months ago, before I learned Soul Vision, I couldn't have done that. I would have been a basket case. I would have cried. I would have been in total torment.

Winged Wolf: Okay, let's talk about the change in you after you began placing your attention on the Third Eye. Do you agree that living with your attention there, stopped you from manipulating another person's energy?
Questioner: Yes.

Winged Wolf: Simply by placing your attention on the Third

Eye, you stopped a negative pattern in your life. That's pretty amazing, isn't it?

Questioner: It really was incredible.

Winged Wolf: You are seeing that you don't have to struggle to refine yourself, or to become holy, or to go through any kind of struggle on top of a mountain, or anything else.

Questioner: I've always been into...(hesitates). You know, the mind gets going and then you get into soul searching.

Winged Wolf: Pardon me, "Soul searching"?

Questioner: Well, that is just a term that I have used.

Winged Wolf: We don't want to use that term. Someone will misunderstand and think that Soul searches for things. It doesn't. Soul already IS one with everything. So you see, there is nothing for It to search for.

Questioner: All right then, trying to find out what I had done wrong.

Winged Wolf: Soul doesn't search. The mind searches.

Questioner: (nods) All I can say is it was the most incredible feeling I have felt in this lifetime. To be able to shut out all that mind chatter.

Winged Wolf: And it does. It shuts it off. But then, you say, "Okay, now, as soon as I come back into my everyday state, the business will come rushing in." Yes, it is very possible that it will. So, as you are going along, learning to be Soul - and you know in the beginning you can only be Soul for a few seconds at a time - if you can hold your attention for three seconds, that's something. It's something that you couldn't do before, not consciously. But, as soon as you get out of it, immediately it all rushes back into the mind: Blah, blah, blah. Which means you weren't really there long enough, were you? The mind suddenly falls back into its discussion, back and forth about this and that. But you keep working at it. Gradually, you are living at the Third Eye for five minutes at a time, then you're there ten minutes, then maybe you'll be there a half-hour. But now, when you go back to mentalizing, you know that you were somewhere, in a different space, fully aware of the environment in every situation going on around you. When you came back into the mind, you found it unpleasant. Suddenly, you are so aware of the mental chatter that you weren't involved while in Soul Vision. The tension builds and there's a yearning, which is a hunger to get back as Soul, because you can relax there. There's no inner noise there, and you can look out at situations.

Suppose you had a bad relationship with somebody. You face that person and, as Soul, consciously looking out of the body (it is Soul operating the body rather than mind operating the body) you can look at that individual or that situation and you can clearly see all the circumstances involved, with no question. The knowledge is just there. When the mind is in control, it looks at someone (or something) and dissects them in thought. It is not necessary to dissect a person or situation to understand. As you go along, you observe more and more. You have to learn to LOOK. Look at the world. Look at people. Look at situations. You'll totally know what is going on, if you will just LOOK.

If you mentalize while you are looking at someone, you are verbally - aloud or in word thought - identifying with what you say and relating to it. You may say, "I can see that this person's situation is so and so, because of so and so. I can see this is going on and I can see that is going on." You mull it over...and over, until it becomes a real part of you. Do you get my point?

Questioner: (mumbles something inaudible)

43

Winged Wolf: Let's be very direct. The point I am making is very important.

Questioner: By mulling over another person's problems, you take on the other person's karma.

Winged Wolf: Be careful of using that word karma. It means many things to many people. It is important that we are specific so that we completely understand each other.

Questioner: Would predicament be a better word?

Winged Wolf: Yes, but not necessarily the actual predicament. By identifying with another's problems, and you do so when you get into mulling a person over in your mind, the symptoms that you have been analyzing in them, become your symptoms. You take on the symptoms, maybe not in the same problem area, but the energy of the same problem. This process begins the moment you begin to mull it over.

Questioner: Frightening.

Winged Wolf: Do you see what you are doing?

Questioner: (hesitates)

Winged Wolf: By saying that it's frightening, you have latched onto fear because of what we are discussing. If you do that, you are creating a disorder in your energy field, disrupting your personal flow by your relationship to what we are discussing.

Questioner: I'm confused.

Winged Wolf: I am talking to you as Soul. I want you to listen as Soul, from your Third Eye center, otherwise you have latched onto the symptoms of the lesson, without learning anything. We are discussing living as Soul in a physical body versus being controlled by the mind, which is a computer.

Questioner: Where do emotions come into play?

Winged Wolf: (hesitates) Good point. Before we get on with this, let's identify emotions.

Questioner: Love, hate, fear, sorrow, joy.

Winged Wolf: Yes, those are emotions, but where do they come from?

Questioner: From the mind.

Winged Wolf: How did the mind get them?

Questioner: I don't know.

Winged Wolf: Of course you do. Please go slowly so that we can get it right.

Questioner: Emotions come from our experiences.

Winged Wolf: Exactly. Emotions come from our experiences and where do our experiences come from?

Questioner: (mumbles something inaudible)

Winged Wolf: Experiences are collected memories, aren't they? Memory makes up the mental programming within the mind. The mind is a computer. Memory is the software. Emotions are the buttons that bring the software into play. When you listen to someone's experience from your mind, an emotional button in your computer is pushed to sound an alarm, or to relate to one of your memories. Thus, you identify with the speaker. You have joined energy, so to speak.

**   When you pass judgment on another person or a situation, you set up resistance between you and that person or**

object. You are passing judgment from your own core, not from their core. Can you see...what you mentalize about another person is what you see in yourself, good or bad? Do you understand.

Questioner: That resistance is set up?

Winged Wolf: Resistance binds you to that which you resist.

Questioner: So what do I do?

Winged Wolf: You have to give up passing judgment, which sets up resistance.

Questioner: By living as Soul, with the attention at the Third Eye.

Winged Wolf: Yes! As you go along, you learn more and more about LOOKING. As we said before, you have to learn to LOOK. LOOK at the world. LOOK at people. You will totally know them if you will simply LOOK at them from the viewpoint of Soul.
    If you will look out as Soul, looking out of the body, using the body's eyes as a vehicle to accomplish this, using the body to touch things without mentalizing about what you are touching (If you have an itch, scratch it, but don't mentalize about why you have the itch), and go about your business, you are aware. You know everything, right then. And if there's a reason for the itch that's important to know, you'll know that, too. You simply know. Soul perceives it. Soul perceives feeling. It perceives energy. When you walk into a room as Soul, you know whether or not it is comfortable energy, or it uncomfortable. And if it's uncomfortable, listen to your body as it tightens up. Get the heck out! Don't stay there and mentalize and say, "Maybe I'm wrong. Maybe so and so doesn't mean it." Well, who cares who means what. If it isn't comfortable and right for you, don't do it.
    We have gotten used to denying ourselves our truth. We

know something but somebody else has expressed an opinion or, society has given us an idea to live by, or our schools have given us something, or our family, our parents, our brothers and our sisters, or our teachers. Everybody has influenced us. We've hidden all these little bits and pieces of information inside the brain. We say to ourselves, "Well, I feel this way, but maybe I don't have a right to feel that, so maybe they are right," which brings us to something else.

It is really difficult to know if you are right about something when you are living in the mind. This is because you will take every situation that comes to you and you will throw an opposite out to contradict or argue with what you determine. The mind is the most unreliable decision maker. When you try to find your comfort zones from mind, you are going to be in trouble. You can't say, "Well, I didn't feel comfortable in there and I left," because if you do, the mind will ask, "Why didn't you feel comfortable?" Then you have to answer inside of yourself, "Because this and so and so was going on, and I was thinking about that, and this was going on." Do you get my point?

All of this is mental junk! Your mental junk didn't feel comfortable with somebody else's mental junk. You've got to go into a place as Soul, to know if you feel comfortable or not, otherwise you are being influenced by this, that, and the other thing, that is going on. What is really you? If you want to know what is you, put your attention on the Third Eye. The Third Eye is the seat of Soul and that is the real you. When you live from this point in your body, a very special thing occurs. You look out at the world and you realize that the world is you, too. You realize that everything that you are looking at is you. This is also how you come into a state of knowing God, because you are a part of God, as well. But these ideas are merely words and concepts until you learn to live from the Third Eye center yourself, then these words are realized through your own experience. Isn't it amazing? You actually realize God, just through living at the Third Eye center. You suddenly realize that you are everything. Everyone you meet, you're them. So you can communicate with anybody on any level, in any situation, because you are what they are, and they recognize something. They don't know what it is, but they recognize something. And, what they are recognizing is that they are what they feel from you, so there is comfort. It's so exciting, I can't tell you, but you are feeling it, you are experiencing it, and it is getting bigger, and bigger and bigger inside of you. The more you do it, live as Soul from the center of your forehead, the greater it gets.

Questioner: And it is a much more comfortable place to be.

Winged Wolf: Yes.

Questioner: It's not tiring. My days are so full. I am three times more busy, and I am three times less tired.

Winged Wolf: You are energized. The more you live as Soul, the greater the energy that flows through you. The energy becomes so great, which is why you must outflow it. You have to channel it through some area of activity. You cannot merely sit in a chair and watch television all day. You couldn't do it and live as Soul. You could not contain the energy. If you tried to contain the energy and it got bigger and bigger in you, you would die. You would burn up. You would consume yourself. You have to outflow it. You have to get out into the world and move and touch things. Everything you touch is "touched" with that energy. You cannot contain it, because it grows greater and greater.

Questioner: I used to require at least eight hours, if not nine, of sleep. If I worked an eight hour day, I was exhausted by the time I got home, and then all I wanted to do was sit and read or do something that required little energy, even on weekends. Now I get five or six hours of sleep. I have been working more than eight hours a day. I still do things in the evening and I am working on Saturdays and Sundays. It is so unbelievable to me to look at where I was a few months ago, to where I am now. I just absolutely love it.

Winged Wolf: Getting freed up.

Questioner: Oh, yes!

Winged Wolf: And your asthma, is it better?

Questioner: Much better. I am getting up early in the morning and walking an hour before I go to work. My walks are meaningful. I now see and hear things in nature that I would have walked right past before.

Winged Wolf: Isn't that wonderful. All of your senses are exaggerated. So you see, all of life is enhanced by Soul Vision, not just this little area that we call spirituality, because all life becomes a spiritual experience. Brushing your teeth is a spiritual experience when you are living as Soul.

Questioner: For me, I have a different feeling of my own body. It's like realizing that I am brushing my hair and my teeth, taking care of the body I am wearing.

Winged Wolf: And you like yourself, don't you?

Questioner: Yes! I actually look in the mirror and feel good about myself.

Winged Wolf: And you feel good in the morning. You wake up and feel happy, ready to go.
Questioner: Yes, and not, "Oh, gosh, do I really have to get up and go this morning?"

Winged Wolf: This is wonderful!

Questioner: And there is an amazing difference in my relationship with my household pets.

Winged Wolf: The critters really like you, as Soul.

Questioner: I feel closer to them.

Winged Wolf: And you can deal with difficult situations at work. All kinds of traumas can come up, and, if you are as Soul, it just works through, doesn't it?

Questioner: Yes, and I am actually enjoying my work so much more now than I was before. I used to get frustrated so easily, feel put off and get angry about something.

Winged Wolf: Now there is no frustration.

Questioner: No, everything comes and goes with a smoothness to it.

Winged Wolf: This doesn't mean that you cannot use your emotions, as expressions. We are here as Soul in a physical body. We use the tools at hand. It is not the other way around. When a person lives as mind, they are controlled by emotions, by anger, lust, greed, fear and so on. All these are mind passions. Now, living as Soul (from the Third Eye center, which is the seat of Soul in the body), you can use your emotions to get a point across to someone, without being consumed by the emotion you are using. You are using the emotion, instead of the emotion using you.

Questioner: I was afraid of anger for a long time, because I felt I would actually be physically sick after I got angry. It was like a venom or a poison.

Winged Wolf: It is a poison!

Questioner: And so, I was afraid to vent any anger. Now I can and I don't feel badly.

Winged Wolf: Let's backup a moment and talk about this anger. If an emotion, a strong feeling, is thrown out into the environment, it actually has an effect in the environment and

it has an effect on the person who felt it. When you feel strong emotion like that, if it is a sustained emotion, over a period of time (and anger can be silent or unspoken, or even feelings of despair), there will be an effect on a person's health.

Questioner: Despair is anger?

Winged Wolf: Yes. Despair is anger turned inward at yourself, or anger suppressed. It's like, "Oh, I'm stuck with this situation in life. Poor me." That's despair. When we do that, it begins to make us sick. It turns the energy molecules in our body in certain chaotic directions and little knots begin to form in our bodies. Each one of us has vulnerable parts in our body, according to our genealogy and lifestyle. Some people are vulnerable in their knees. Their anger and sustained emotions will form little clots of nerve entanglements in their knees, or in their joints, their backs, their organs, or their head. You know, people who get headaches or different things suffer from this twisted, pinched nerve effect. A little gang of muscles gather (motions to the shoulders) and so people carry their shoulders unevenly, instead of straight. All of these physical discomforts occur through strong, sustained emotion, brain damage.

When we learn to live as Soul, via Soul Vision (Third Eye), the damage in our brains begins to heal. Brain damage comes from sustained emotion, strong sustained emotion, where it's happening over and over. It comes from feelings that are held inside, not expressed or expressed and not released fully. Now, we're not talking about a little flair here and a week later another little flair. That doesn't do anything. That's just puff. Nothing. We are talking about sustained feeling. Feelings that people carry inside of themselves, grudges and such.

Questioner: What makes a person carry a grudge or, rather, susceptible to hanging onto strong feeling?

Winged Wolf: How you hang onto something, as well as the depth of how you hang onto it, is presented by a person's individual myth. Each person has a story that he has been concocting since birth. This story, built through childhood and through adult life, has a lot of feeling connected to it. The story itself protects from fear, or from situations that make him uncomfortable. It gets quite complicated. The story has to be complicated to cover all the bases that fear lurks behind.

This story, which is actually the individual's personal myth, invented by him, is woven with the fibers of sustained feelings. And, mostly, they are negative feelings-concerns over this and that, whether someone is going to love or think kindly of him, or not, all kinds of worries, fears, guilt and the like. After a time, all of these negative feelings assemble together in a clump within our nervous system. Sore muscles are usually caused from physical strain of lifting something heavy. We are talking about pinched nerves. However, our nervous system is all intertwined and knotted together from emotional strain. After a period of time, disease sets in. It's like rubbing, rubbing, rubbing the cat's fur the wrong way, every day, all day long. Eventually, that cat is going to get sick. Do you see, these little nerves are being irritated?

Now, the moment you stop the irritation, the moment you begin to live as Soul for even one minute a day, the disease begins to remiss. The nerves gathered about an organ, a bone, or somewhere in the brain, begin to loosen. For that one minute a day, the nerves relax and are not hurting each other. This one minute a day comes from living with your attention on the Third Eye.

Questioner: Why?

Winged Wolf: Because, when the attention is at the Third Eye, you are living as Soul. The mind is quiet. There is none of that continual chatter going on inside of the brain. There is no conflict, no reason for the nerves to be upset, which causes the disease. That one minute a day, those little nerves have a chance to relax and the energy cells in our body have a moment to go back to normal movement. We are using an example here, because one moment a day probably wouldn't be enough to reverse a disease. The energy flow would begin to get into some kind of movement again and then we'd stop it with the continuation of sustained negative emotion. But, as you develop more as Soul, living in the body, the more you can stay with this Third Eye viewpoint. I have witnessed miraculous results. You can actually reverse cancer. You can reverse any kind of a physical ailment. You can reverse any kind of a negative situation. People can be uplifted from poverty, because Soul's natural state is abundance. People who are caught in crime are in this pattern. People who have one bad thing after another happen to them are in this pattern. Once the pattern is broken, the healing starts. It is broken the moment you have your attention on the Third Eye, when you are living as Soul in the body. When you can get to the point when you can live as Soul for a half-hour a day, a minute here and a minute there, you are really mending your body and your life. You start to see light coming from your flesh, a lightness. You feel the energy building in you and you begin feeling really good. There is a joy that starts to happen inside of you that has no explanation. It's a blissful feeling, not dependent on anything or anyone. You are living freely for the first time. Health is a by-product of this freedom. It all goes together. So you see, the benefits of learning to see through the Third Eye are astounding. And, to top it off, if you were to take an I.Q. test, you would find that your I.Q. would probably have jumped - twenty, thirty, maybe forty points.

Scientists are always telling us that we use only three to five percent of our brains. Why is that? We only use a small portion of our brains because of all of the mental chatter that is going on all the time. There is so much inner conversation, yakity yak, that the brain becomes stupid. It can't function properly because the constant conversation going on inside of it produces conflict, negative concerns. It's full of buttons, busying a person's life with foul images and worries. After all, the brain is computer like. The software it contains can be likened to education, complicated by a person's individual myth. Someone says something and a button is pushed. A relationship is summoned from the myth and the result is a muddled mess.

Once the mind quiets down, once you are living as Soul, seeing through the Third Eye, then the brain is able to function more wholly. You are able to use more of your brain, like you can use more of a room once the clutter is removed. Your brain will become smarter. Your body will become healthier, and your life will become happier. You don't have to sit in a lotus position, meditating for twenty years to have it happen. The effects of living as Soul are instantaneous, right HERE, right NOW. The only reason you need a teacher is to show you what phenomena is possible for you, and to help you break away the crust, or recognize your myth, which keeps you from living this state of joy, freedom and abundance. If the mind were not so strongly set from so many years of myth-building, a teacher would not be important. I had a ruthless teacher, who ripped away everything that I had and held it up for me to see, even the halo I had invented to make myself seem good and important. She was shocking. In CIRCLE OF POWER, I talk about her picking up on something I was feeling and thinking (resistance) and, she threw me face down in the mud. I mean, I had mud oozing through my teeth. My apprentices look at me as a pussy cat. But, there does come a point, in the latter part of an apprentice's relationship with a teacher, where she has to be pushed through the eye of a needle, and it is always shocking. (Pause.)

Being pushed through the eye of the needle is a time when you are living so impeccably as Soul that you are able to live omni-presently, that you can experience what most people call phenomena, and live it as ordinary reality, because it is not phenomena at all. It is only phenomena to the mind. One's mind set (myth) designates what is phenomena or what is ordinary or normal. Living from Soul there is no such thing as phenomena.

What you call phenomena is natural freedom and every-one was born with a capacity for it. We have been tricked out of it through our lives. Now people are learning to get it back. Getting it back does not mean learning anything. It is merely the process you have to go through in order to get enough looseness in the mind, enough flexibility so that your assemblage point can shift and stay shifted. What holds a person up is looking at limitation from a mental point of view. When you do that, you say, "Oh, well, I can't do this. I can't do that." You know, that's the mind saying, "This is the reason I can't live as Soul. I'd have to give up my family." That's a bunch of silly chatter. You don't have to give up anything except baggage that weighs you down and that doesn't have anything to do with anybody else.

People usually look outside of themselves to hang the blame for something on everybody else, or the praise for that matter. You, know, "God is directing my life." You are di-recting your life. Soul is a part of God so nothing is happen-ing outside of you. There is nothing greater than Soul. Soul is not God, but Soul is a part of God. Living as Soul means that you accept responsibility for yourself. That's a biggie! That's enough to scare many people off right there. They say, "Oh, my gosh; I have to accept responsibility for myself?" Yes, you do, but it's not as frightening as you think.

If you are living as Soul, you're perspective of life changes and that in itself changes everything around you. You have a different, more responsible, more real and fulfill-ing relationship with people as Soul than you do than when experiencing life from between the ears, from the mind-computer. As Soul, you have a warm, loving, compassionate relationship with people. You might say you have that now, living from mind, but it's not the same. Mostly, your happi-ness is based on people and things. When you are living from mind, you have a conditional love. "I love you for this, but I don't love you because of that. I think you are a wonderful person, but you have this problem. I can accept this part of you, but I can't accept that part of you." As Soul, the love

you feel is unconditional. You accept wholeheartedly because you are THAT!

We are talking about freedom. Wholeheartedness is
freedom. Please pay attention. This is big time stuff. Life
doesn't end on top of the mountain. It begins on top of the
mountain. My apprentices move to the top of the mountain
right now and learn to explore from the top, not scratching
to get to the top of the mountain twenty years from now.
How many people make it to the top like that? They become
so mind distracted along the way, they never get there. The
business of meditating, fighting yourself to hold the thoughts
from your mind, does not work for very many people. The
reason many people can't succeed this way is because, any-
time you have to fight something, as soon as you let go, it is
just going to rush in at you. Thoughts will bombard you as
soon as you complete your daily meditation. Life is a living
meditation. All you have to do is get your attention to the
Third Eye and there is no thought. But you have full faculty of
mind, fuller than you ever had. It's amazing! There is no
work to it really.

*Questioner: Yes, we always had this preconceived idea that it
took such a great amount of work. (Hesitates.) You're not
saying that the mind becomes useless.*

Winged Wolf: No! No! You're not paying attention. I said
before that the mind becomes more brilliant, because there is
no conflict to short-circuit the functioning of the brain. You
will learn, however, that thought is over-rated.

Questioner: But one does not really ever stop thinking.

Winged Wolf: Thinking, as most people know it, becomes less
and less. They know thinking as mind chatter. Instead of
thinking like that you will come into direct perception where,
as Soul, you will look at something and know all about it;
that is, you know the energy involved and make your decisions and choices from there.

It doesn't matter how estranged somebody's life is, when they start doing it, they come into balance again. I've seen so-called average people enhance their lives in a most exciting way, fulfilling their dreams from Soul Vision. I've also seen really crazy people - depressed, paranoid, suicidal people turn their lives completely around simply because they began to focus on the Third Eye and became interested in the effects they were having. These people became like a hound after a rabbit. It's very interesting.

There was this one person. She wasn't crazy, but she was a diagnosed MPD (multiple personality). She merged and become whole. She went from more than thirty personalities and merged them all. Can you imagine that?

Questioner: How did she do that?

Winged Wolf: She left notes for the various personalities and taught each of them about living as Soul and how to do it. Today, she is one of the most wonderful people I've ever met, and she is an apprentice. If she decides to pursue this path and see it through, I have no doubt that she will become a very powerful shaman.

So you see, I really have nothing to do with it. Each individual must do the work herself. I am merely a guide. I see things and I point them out.

Questioner: Do you know they can turn themselves around when you meet them.

Winged Wolf: Oh, no. Sometimes when they come to me, I look at them and shake my head. I can see that they are in big time trouble. "Oh, my goodness! This is big time!" I tell myself. But then, there's something that happens, even to people with great problems. It doesn't matter if the person is schizophrenic. It doesn't matter if a person has any kind of mental disease. It doesn't matter what the problem is. When a person starts to live as Soul, everything lines up. I have seen the most incredible changes in people. I don't do it. They live as Soul. It's really wonderful! There isn't anybody who can't do it. Just imagine if all of them become shaman! Becoming shaman means that you live in freedom and that you honor and respect the freedom of all life.

A shaman never manipulates. Never! The penalty for manipulation is really hard on somebody that does it. You've seen the results. When you try to manipulate a situation, what happens? It always backfires. You might make progress with it for a short time and then, sooner or later, the situation all falls apart and it comes back on you. "Oh, wow! I was doing good there for awhile, but nothing is working for me anymore." That's because you were playing with the psychic forces. As Soul, you carry inside of you everything that you ever wanted.

As Soul, it's natural for me to sit down at the computer and write a book. I don't have to sit there and make an outline and worry about this, and worry about that. I AM what I want to do. All I have to do is to sit down and DO it. Do you see? It's like, once you learn to drive a car and have experience at the wheel, you don't get into a car and say, "Now, I have to turn the key. Now I have to put it in neutral. Now, I put my foot on the brake." You know! You are already a driver; so, you just go ahead and do it. That's how you live as Soul. You make your choices every step of the way, but it's not a mental, mulling it over kind of choice. It's not, "Shall I go this way or that way?" You look at something with perfect clarity. You perceive the energy of it, and you KNOW. And you DO. And, it's good. And, it's uplifting to the whole, because it can't be any other way. It has to be uplifting to the whole but you did it as Soul. Isn't that great! But now, dialogue with me. Let's make this crystal clear. Let's get into it. Don't be afraid to ask anything that would question this Soul Vision thing deeper. Any kind of question is valid.

Questioner: I found it very simple and yet, very complex when I started.

Winged Wolf: That's what it is. It is so simple, but it's not easy because you have to let go and release some old business.

Questioner: And, because of my Eastern religion disciplines, I would automatically close my eyes. I wouldn't even know they were closed. I would sit down to do the exercises and I would notice my eyes closed. So, it has been a totally different way of viewing.

Winged Wolf: Yes. First of all, you are accustomed to meditating with your eyes closed. And, the first thing you do, when you get your eyes closed is view the image you have in there. Your view of the image captures you and you trip off somewhere. You're gone into the inner planes, so to speak. As Soul, you have to be right here. Right now. Of course, there are many HERES and NOWS. There are "heres and nows" simultaneous with "heres and nows" in other planes and dimensions. But, in the beginning, it is very, very important for you to be grounded to the earth, to learn to live with life rather than escaping from life, to live in the present moment, in this moment, in this frame of time that you are in, this environment.

People are always trying to escape life. "Oh, I know "after life" is going to be better. Many religions teach that, you know. Some religions teach about the joys of living in heaven, and then there are those who focus on reincarnation and cliche type thinking, "Well, if I don't do well this time, I'll come back and get another crack at it." The Eastern religions are notorious for that. You look all over India. They have no respect for life at all. "Well, so and so will come back as..." you know, and when somebody comes back as something that society over there considers valuable, well then, there is a little respect for the life. Reincarnation, the ideas that people have about reincarnation are very silly... wasteful and silly. It doesn't matter who you were. You are NOW the sum total of everyone you have ever been. There is no point in looking backwards. There is no point in looking forwards... because tomorrow you are going to be an evolvement of the person you are today. So, you see, we always drag ourselves around with ourselves, which is why we don't need to go delving into that. It's the mind that likes to play with those ideas. This is why people cannot do this work on their own. The teacher is necessary to guide the individual, because the mind is continually stretching here and there, saying, "Let's go over there a little bit, and let's explore over here a little bit." Well, as a teacher and guide, I can feel it when my apprentices do that. There is a little tentacle, a connection as Soul that says, "Oh, Michael's going off over that way."

Questioner: I was very much into disciplines. I wore them like a badge. They became an identity and it was a place to go and it was, I thought, me. Just the process of letting this go, even if I hadn't gone into Soul Vision, even if I hadn't gone into a wonderful place, which I have, it was so remarkable for me simply to let that go; to be in the here and now and really be free and in power.

Winged Wolf: The point I want to get across is that functioning with your eyes open, makes you aware of the environment right there in front of you. You're looking out as Soul, and simply looking without mental comment about what you see. You're learning to LOOK. Life is a walking meditation. You don't have to sit down in a chair, or sit cross-legged on the floor, to discipline yourself. You can do that, but it is not necessary. All you have to do is walk around LOOKING. Once in a while scratch the center of your forehead, so that you feel a little tingling sensation there. You will be reminded to return to the Third Eye center. People wander off even with their eyes open, engaging in fantasies and daydreams. You might have wandered across the street while you were walking up the street. In your imagination, you are over there, or visiting somebody over here, or you're back at work, or you're at home chatting with your husband, wife, or your children, or whatever, instead of being right here, NOW. Looking out right here, is where the bliss is. Right here. And my, it is blissful! It's where the freedom is...right here! And, when you become accustomed to freedom right here, and you're really looking out and participating in the world - from this moment, in this moment - a whole new life opens up. And something else happens, as well.

I get letters from apprentices saying, "I feel like I'm in a void." Okay! I see heads nodding everywhere. This is the beginning. If you allow the mind to get into it at this point, it'll say, "Oh, I'm so alone. I feel so alone." Please pay attention. This feeling is the mind remembering the fact that the void was there. It's the mind looking at its memory of the void and becoming frightened. The mind becomes frightened because the void is the nothing space, THE NO THING SPACE. Even though you relate on a physical level to earthly things all around, and to people, and to animals, and to plants, it is a NO THING SPACE while you're doing this. This NO THING SPACE is where the miracle activity, or so-called miracle activity takes place. It is not really miracle activity at all. It is only miracles from the mind's viewpoint, that of remembering the NO THING SPACE. So you see, if you are bold and adventuresome, and allow yourself to adventure into the void, become accustomed to it, you're really free. You can do anything! Your life becomes a living miracle. You become a healer. A healer is a person living in balance, which means living a life of abundance and joy.

Questioner: In my practices with Eastern Religions, I never experienced this. I had removed myself from the world.

Winged Wolf: You were so busy holding thoughts away, struggling, that nothing could happen. You couldn't sense the void, because what you were doing was imposing your will against your mind. There is no value to it at all.

Questioner: The value that I found was primarily using it as a tool to relate to something else.

Winged Wolf: Are you talking about contemplation?

Questioner: No, just letting go of thought and then having a feeling of something else...Great Spirit, whatever.

Winged Wolf: But, see, that's still a mental concept.

Questioner: My point, which was in a sense, partly NO THING. (Pause.) Well, it seemed like it to me, because it was on the way, or in the process. There was a relationship. There was this process to get to the relationship. But, now that I have experienced NO THING, I see how very different it is.

Winged Wolf: It is very different. God is a mental concept, in any form. It's an invention of the mind, and yet, you are part of God. Each one of us is a part of God. This is a different subject. Right now, we are discussing the mind. The mind is capable of inventing many things. My point is, you don't need to invent things in order to have an exciting life. I can do whatever I want. I don't invent it with my mind. As Soul, you know what you are, what you want, that which suits you, without putting together words inside of your head to say that, or images. This creative visualization thing, it's a waste of energy. It's a detour. It runs you down the trail, without the intended results. You can visualize something and start pulling it in your direction, but then, the image suddenly erupts, changes somehow, because of a tiny glitch in your emotional body, and all your efforts go hay-wire. The whole situation gets messed up and then you say, "Well, I got this but it's not what I thought I'd get. Not what I wanted." The real reason it didn't come out right is because you were conjuring, or messing around with energy, which is witch-craft. When an individual is living as Soul, they don't func-tion that way. Not that witchcraft is bad, or any other reli-gion is bad, and witchcraft is a religion. It has nothing to do with good or bad. My point is, why have detours, when you don't need a detour? If you choose personally to have a detour, that's fine. That's your business. I don't choose to have any detours. I don't need it. When one gets to the point where they are living as Soul, enough of the time, then your

whole life JUST IS. IT'S PRESENTED. Life outwardly presents what you are. You DO. You can't just sit in a chair and do nothing. You have to DO. That's what life is about. We are here in a physical body to learn to live as Soul. Physical life is about DOING. It's about participating. Life as Soul is active, not passive. It's giving, and it's releasing!

PART 3

A TASTE OF SPRING

I looked up from the material I had been reading. "I bet the tea is cold," I said, rising from my seat next to Alana. Although she had not said anything about my book, I sensed she was very happy with me. "It'll take a moment. I have to warm it up," I called out. I slid the pot over the hot cooking stone and stoked the coals beneath it. It amazed me how simply Alana lived, and even more amazing was how comfortable her life style was, even without the amenities of modern life.

I heard her say something that was not quite audible and turned around.

"I said, you couldn't live this way. It's not for you, Heather."

"I wouldn't miss civilization that much," I rebutted.

"Yes, you would. You like to turn a handle and have hot water come out, and flip a switch for light."

"Looks like you have plenty of light, without flipping a switch." I was commenting on how her radiance filled the room.

"Living simply has its benefits," Alana said.

"Meaning?"

"It forces me to rely on my own resources. I don't have any switches to flip."

I laughed. "Are you manipulating energy?" I teased.

"No, I am being myself, which gives me what I require. When you are ready to live simply, you will do the same for yourself."

"I am ready to live simply now," I said.

"No, you're not. Your work requires you to use your energy in other ways."

I removed the pot from the heating stone and poured the dandelion tea into both our cups, carried them to Alana's sleeping rug and handed her one.

I held my cup between the palms of my hands, gazing into the amber liquid. Did Alana want dandelion tea because she was having trouble with her digestion?

"I asked for dandelion tea because it has the taste of Spring," she said, answering my unspoken question. "And because of the communication it provides us today." She lifted the letters from her sleeping rug that I had taken from my mailbox in Arizona. "Your mail is wonderful. I can see you have quite a challenge, and that it prods you forward, as well."

I said that that was true, that my apprentices were always nudging me through their desire to become shaman. As I spoke, it occurred to me that Alana was leaving me because I no longer needed her in the same way.

"There are many ways to serve," Alana broke into my silence. "The service that I will now give will boost your energies a thousand fold." She paused, studying the perplexity in my eyes. "I am giving you the gift of our lineage, a total merger of energies."

"Would you tell me about our lineage?" I asked eagerly. She had never spoken to me about her roots.

"I was born into the Lakota tribe as Alana Naomi, daughter of Naomi Setari, who was the daughter of Setari Patiri, daughter of Patiri Jaminar, who was the daughter of Jaminar Polita, daughter of Polita Heatshe, who was the daughter of Heatshe Natsa....."

Alana stopped speaking as I quickly looked around for a pen and paper to write on. "Don't worry," she said, "my memory will be yours when I leave. All the stories I contain will be your stories." I stopped fidgeting and gazed into her eyes. "You already have access to much of me - my knowledge, my wisdom and my native language, but there is much more." The native language Alana referred to was a peculiar incidence that began one evening while I was chatting with some apprentices in the living room of my Arizona home. In the middle of a sentence, I suddenly began babbling in another language. "She's speaking in tongues," one apprentice said. I laughed at the ridiculousness of the comment, however the odd language continued intermittently. Later that night I woke up from a deep sleep, babbling. I turned on the light and wrote the words down, phonetically as best I could. I even held them in front of a mirror to see if there were a reversed meaning, but there wasn't. I found out later that the language was Sioux, a gift from my teacher to satisfy my complaint that I felt I would never be able to learn a second language because of my dyslexia (which I had had since childhood). As the days, weeks, months, a year went by, the language developed in me. I no longer spoke in one word syllables, but in whole sentences and paragraphs. The language instilled in me became quite complex. I frequently use this language around animals, who seem to respond to it better than English.

Alana began to speak in Sioux to me, explaining the nature of a shaman's gifts, which she said were rooted in love. "Surely, you have something in the book you are writing about love," she said, politely prodding me.

I picked up the computer print-out and thumbed through it until I came to the discourse on LOVE. "Shall I read it to you?" I asked.

"Please."

LOVE

There are many types and levels of love. A parent loves a child as God loves a child, whereas a child love the parent as one who would love God. In every lover-beloved relationship, there is apprentice the lover and God the adept; thus God, the lover, is always the figure to be emulated in the relationship, just as the apprentice (the beloved) always looks to the teacher, the lover. The difference between the child and the apprentice is that the child unknowingly becomes the parent, whereas the apprentice, in order to receive that which the adept has to give, must consciously merge with her teacher.

This upsets the apprentice, makes her feel vulnerable but there is no way to attain the higher consciousness without merging with the teacher. The "merging" that we speak of is a merging of Soul, wherein two distinct bodies and personalities become one as Soul.

This is frightening to most people, and rightly so. It was certainly a frightening idea and feeling to me. I was terrified of becoming ONE with my teacher and I fought my love for her, just as the Persian Sufi

Rumi suffered in order to merge with his teacher Shamis Tabriz.

You say, Alana, my teacher was shaman and Rumi was not. Shaman is not a term used to define a religion or a religious sect, although there are some races who would have you believe so. The word shaman relates to a being of higher consciousness, one who is no longer fettered to the ordinary world and, yet, lives a life of joy and abundance on all levels, being totally free and omnipresent. Rumi was such a man. Milarepa, whom I wrote about in SHAMAN OF TIBET, while earmarked in history as a Buddhist, was also a shaman, or one bearing the description of one, as was Guatama Buddha.

"Love is looking out at the world.
Looking out means viewpoint of
Soul."

Flight of Winged Wolf
Page 138

"There is always risk to a gift. The
receiver does not always have the
same interest in mind as the
giver."

Circle of Power
Page 109

Alana had opened one of the letters I had received and was reading it. "This man talks about love differently. He tells you about his need for his wife, and wants to know how to live happily with her."

I turned the page, and began to read again.

HOME AS A MEDICINE LODGE

Treat your home as you would the most sacred place on earth. It is the place where your body dwells, and your body is a conveyance for Soul. If you are married and/or have children, your home is also the home of your family, the more who reside with you, the greater expression of Soul, if you are living as Soul. By living as Soul, I mean that all who dwell within are living with their attention on the Tisra Til, at the center of the forehead. It is okay even if only one in the household resides as Soul. One individual as Soul is a vortex of harmony, which, by its nature, spirals outward to form a protective field of energy around the dwelling and those who reside there. This is what is meant by making your home a medicine lodge. A medicine lodge contains only purified energy. Here are a few suggestion for preserving the sanctity of your home.

1. Speak only kind words in your home. If you must say something unkind, go outdoors where the wind and other elements will assist you in dissipating your negative feelings. Better yet, dig a hole in the ground and shout your obscenities there. Then bury them with a prayer of gratitude to the earth.

2. *Choose your television and radio wisely.* Don't watch upsetting news or dramas that leave you agitated emotionally. If something disturbing comes on television, switch channels, or turn it off. Television and radio are presented in your home by a series of energized wave lengths. The images projected - visual and sound - are actual proportions of the energy projected. Do you want crime energies - fear, incest, rape - in your home? Notice how your family's emotions are hooked by their entertainment, and notice how their moods change and affect the general dynamics within the home.

3. *Invite people into your home that will add to the grace of your medicine lodge.* Never invite someone because you feel you should when your intuition says NO.

4. *Live impeccably in your home,* treating all that you do within it as something acted out within a sacred medicine lodge. When you return home from a busy day, your home lodge will be a place of healing, where you will feel nurtured and renewed.

SEX

The most destructive relationship is the sexual relationship. There is a difference between making love and sharing the intimacy of ecstatic union with one who shares your life (or one who you intend to share life with) and "having sex" with someone who holds little importance in your life. When this latter circumstance occurs, the orgasm experienced is an extortion that produces a jolt of lewd expression in the aura of the persons involved, lowering their vibrations to flaunt murky colors in their auras. Of course, anyone who experiences sex for sex only already has naturally low vibrations. They live in debauchery, the forerunner to poverty consciousness. When you meet such a person, even though he/she may appear attractive, you will automatically feel a discomfort in your lower chakras. Feelings of odd excitement, repulsion, and distrust often follow.

Many marriage partners use sex to manipulate each other. The wife may withhold her body in anger, and the husband may take her body in anger. Sex is often used to smooth things over when there has been an argument. This type of performance is an effort to cover up difficulties, as well as an effort to take control of a negative situation, power struggles. If marriage partners would discover how to live as Soul, they would develop in themselves the ecstatic art of making love. This involves romance, courtship, respect, admiration and mutual love. Any manipulation of your partner's feelings, is a violation of spiritual law and reduces the union to a sexual encounter. There is no need to plot your partner's response to your loving actions. If your actions occur from pure love, the results will be impeccable. Glorious!

Likewise, children should not be born out of sex, but rather out of making love. In this way, the vibration that enlivens the seed into fertilization will enliven Soul, minimizing the karmic burden of birth.

[NOTE: Tantric Yoga, in its undistorted form, teaches the principles of making love. Tantric Yoga books in the marketplace today are mostly misinterpretations. The Tantras are encyclopedias of esoteric Hindu knowledge that denote the creation of the universe, devotion to God, spiritual exercise, rituals, and the magical powers of life. One of the magical powers of life is sex, which has the ability to create new life form. The application of sex as a magical power is where opportunists have misled the public.]

"And what would you say to this same man about being a parent to his children?" Alana asked, gazing at me affectionately. I looked back at her for a long moment. While she was not the mother of my flesh, she was the mother who nurtured my spirit. The gifts of her difficult teachings had always strengthened and uplifted me. I turned the page. The next piece of paper held comments I had written about parenting.

PARENTING

Children are little people, meaning they are Soul beginning a life cycle of experience. As the body grows to maturity, so it is that Soul's experiences are meant to mature; that is, Soul is meant to dominate the body and mind to experience life. Children should be encouraged to discover their impeccable nature, the part of themselves that lives in joy, and to recognize that when there is conflict there is mental imbalance, meaning that emotions are battling between person and person, or between groups of people and groups of people. Children should be taught that controlling emotions springs from fear of doing without or fear of not getting their so called fair share or sentimentality (which is fearing/feeling loss, or fearing lack of pleasure). In like manner they should be taught that pleasure is the flip side of pain and that the two are inseparable, one always follows the other. Most impor-

tantly, they should be taught to live and express themselves, individually as Soul, which is the state of consciousness that utilizes emotion for expression rather than be utilized by emotion. In this way, children will recognize their parent's love as divine or unconditional love, not dependent on behavior or misbehavior, and they will be as secure in life as they are in the home.

If your children were not reared to experience themselves as Soul from the very beginning, no matter. Begin NOW. Since all life exists in the present moment, whatever condition exists in them can be healed by your presence living as Soul. Follow these simple rules:

1. When your child comes to you in anger, recognize that he or she is in pain over some affliction in their body, or their mind. Listen to their complaint, as Soul, compassionately, without attachment or sympathy for their feelings. You will observe a gradual or even a sudden change, a transmutation of the energies through your non-judgment.

2. When your child comes to you seeking pleasure, relief from boredom or loneliness, recognize that

he/she is actually yearning to live as Soul but is caught in the sensory world, which is a part of the experience of youth. Instead of trying to control your child's actions through demands, which rarely succeeds, engage your child's actions constructively. Encourage a project that will consume her attention and teach her responsibility. Healthy tasks include participation in the arts - drawing/painting, playing a musical instrument, a sport or other activity that combines friendship with dexterity and perseverance (such as caring for a horse and learning to ride it).

3. When your child comes to you for nurturing, which is the same as coming to you in anger or pleasure-seeking, pause in what you are doing and give of yourself. Remember that parents and children have, by necessity, a symbiotic relationship. A tree needs the earth to hold its roots so that it may grow; and, likewise, if nothing grows upon the earth, the ground is barren.

Alana was gazing at me with loving eyes when I looked up from the computer print-out of my manuscript. Her feelings were clear. She had nurtured me from the soil she had prepared and, like the tree, I had grown tall. "I am satisfied with you," she said. "And I am grateful to you," I answered. "Then we are friends," she added. "Please read to me what you have written about friendship."

FRIENDSHIP

Friendship is a position of common ground whereby the participants love each other unconditionally and share their love via mutual respect and acceptance. Friends listen to each other and, when they do things together, one uplifts the other. Friends are not competitive. The wishes of one are the desires for the other. Their strengths combine to make each other larger, and stronger, and gentler than they would be individually. To have a friend is to be wealthy beyond words. True friends are treasures and, unlike acquaintances, who come and go in our lives, friends are always with us regardless of distance and length of time between visits. The relationship exists in the present moment and the bond between you is always current.

"People have to learn to stop
communicating with television
and books and instead,
look their compadres in the eye,
Soul to Soul."

Flight of Winged Wolf
Page 110

"True friends are bound
by strings of energy."

Circle of Power
Page 93

"We attract what we love
and what we fear."

Circle of Power
Page 15

"You can tell where a person is coming from by the nature of the feeling she or he gives you."

Circle of Power
Page 15

"We make friends with an animal because there is something in our nature that is compatible with it. There is no big mystery to having a power animal, anymore than there is to having a close human friend. We need only to recognize those aspects of our nature that link us together."

Circle of Power
Page 38

"You know what that means," Alana said, lightly touching my arm.

I knew she was referring to the fact that while she was translating from her body, going to die, that we would always be together. It also meant that I should rejoice in her passing, but how could I? I didn't want her to go. I looked away. There was no way I could hide my feeling from her. "Tell me about our shamanic lineage," I asked.

"The last person I mentioned to you in our lineage was Heatshe Natsa. I stopped there because she is a most important person to you. Like you, she was a teacher for many people. She also wrote information down, not in words, but in images and markings that explained the images. She wrote on tree bark and rocks and clay faces of the earth. Heathe, her brother was also a shaman teacher and record keeper. Together they were very powerful - loving and compassionate teachers. Their personal abilities were enormous and, through them, many were raised to the shaman consciousness. Many of those they taught are awakening today, hundreds of years later." She paused, looking deeply into my eyes. Heatshe and Heathe have merged in identity and are alive today to complete the cycle of their work."

"Heatshe and Heathe," I mumbled, relating to the sound of the names as I repeated them. A slow uneasy feeling crept around my solar plexus and crawled up the base of my spine, settling on the top of my head. Alana was gazing at me, as though my face were unfolding a story. We didn't speak for a long time. Finally, she looked away and opened another of the apprentice letters I had received. After reading it, she commented that the author was concerned about health and healing, and she asked me to read what I had written on the subject.

HEALTH

Health is a state of balance within the body. Balance means that you are considerate of the foods you feed your body, and that you are also considerate of the images you allow into your mind.

Healthy food consists of organic matter that is easily digestible to your body. Originally, one's palate determined what was good for you, but now, tasty food has come to mean spicy, bland, sweet, or tart.

Before the body's sense of taste became distorted by group opinion and by emotional associations (good times, bad times) and tied to taste, one's taste buds discriminately decided if a food was good for you. Primitive people relied on this ability in foraging for food. Animals still rely on it, although domestic animals sense of taste can be somewhat distorted by what their owners have offered them. Thus, if they wander off and find a piece of candy, having had it at home, they will eat it, and possibly in preference to a piece of meat. Animals or people who have never tasted candy, or been taught how "delicious" it is, will usually reject the taste of it. Sweet, sour, and spicy foods are enjoyed through acquired taste.

The tenor of this same statement is true of images

we, as individuals, allow to pass through our minds. Mental images constitute the reflection of the life we live projected into the environment. Of course, people's lack of general discrimination is displayed in our cities crime waves and multitude of sociological difficulties. The home and family were nearly destroyed in our society by the mass shift of mental images brought about by a desire for so-called sexual freedom, as well as freedom of the sexes. Lack of respect for the family and lack of interest from the family has propagated crime. Many people have come to enjoy crime and horror, and this determination is substantiated by what is popular on television and in the movies. Crime, sex and violence make more money than any other subject presented. Newscasters know this, and to gain viewers, they headline the news with chilling rape and child abuse stories. Thus, the cycle is propagated.

Like food that is ingested into the body, ingested images affect the health of the body. If one will monitor the intake of food and images, and eliminate the unhealthy, her body will gain in strength and vigor. A sick body can be enlivened in this way, as well. The difficulty one may have, however, is in the mental conditioning one has established through bad habit.

An easy way to eliminate bad habit is to place the attention on the Third Eye and live there, from the seat of Soul. Then one's choices will naturally be healthy. I am not saying to give up sweet or spicy food. (I also have acquired a taste for it.) I am saying to become aware of how your cravings function, so that they will no longer dominate you. Can you see? In this way, addictions cannot exist.

HEALING

The first question is how badly do you want to be healed? Nearly any healing can be accomplished if you are truly willing to be healed. It may sound silly to suggest that someone is not willing to get well but many people actually identify with their illness. Also, there are those who punish themselves by being sick, for some wrong they "feel" they did to someone. Although they feel the need to be punished, these people either don't realize, or won't admit the cause of their illness to themselves. They simply feel unworthy to be healthy. These people are often the chronically sick. They have one problem and then another, going habitually from one illness to another.

There are others who have had some terrible wrong done to them, have repressed their held back anger and desire to strike back and have become sick. The parts of the body injured, or the type of affliction, usually give a clue as to how the wrongdoing is taking its affect. In the early stages the affliction is localized. Later on the symptoms spread throughout the body. Individuals with a history of allergies may have at one time been trying to protect themselves from an overbearing parent by having an allergic reaction to something that was upsetting for them to perform. As they grew older, the need for an excuse to be themselves (to be authentic) compounded into adult life. This behavior then rules and limits their social life and work. Going to the market becomes a very difficult chore, because of the allergic myth that was perpetuated in their youth.

The more terrible the crime, the more serious the illness. The word "terrible" here is relative to the sensitivity of the individual involved. Many, who as children were rape victims later become obese. They wear their hundreds of overweight pounds as armor to protect themselves from being "attractive." A teenage girl, who displayed affection during a date with a boyfriend, was "date raped." The girl's friends and family criticized the girl instead of the boy, saying that her attractiveness and playfulness was the real cause of her rape. As a result, the girl never again allowed herself to respond passionately in any situation, and her repressed feelings ran the gamut from self-hate to self-guilt to hate again. Consequently, the outward silence she endured became quietly violent, which afflicted the nerves of her body, and eventually compounded into multiple sclerosis.

Methods of healing vary, and the extensiveness of the type of healing tells how well a person is healed. For instance, rarely does a person maintain a healthy body after a cancer is removed. After a while, another cancer appears in the same part of the body or in another part with a similar function because the cause of the disease still exists. Here psychotherapy can help but the difficulty with this is that it often stays focused so long on a problem that the patient cannot heal. It would be like continuing to open a wound rather than allowing it to heal when an anti-septic is administered.

Healing is a matter of cleaning the wound of "cause" so that it, and the effect, can heal simulta-neously. When an individual lives as Soul, from the Third Eye, at the center of the forehead, the emotional images, which have kept the wound infected, cease to exist. The healing begins.

[NOTE: Having an occasional cold in a polluted environment may be necessary to cleanse and purge the impurities from one's system.]

"...the shaman often uses shape
shifts to heal another person
or a situation."

Flight of Winged Wolf
Page 20

"When you feel uncomfortable,
uneasy or in pain; when you feel
in a hurry to solve problems,
under pressure, crowded or
anxious and there seems to be
a lot of noise around you, you are
being affected by the feelings
and desires of what others want
from you."

Flight of Winged Wolf
Page 56

I could feel Alana gazing deeply into me as I looked up from my reading. "Has life been difficult for you recently?" she asked.

Tears came into my eyes and I nodded. Only the week before, my mother had had a massive stroke, and she now lay paralyzed in a hospital. Her distress left me feeling as though part of me had been severed.

"You are feeling the loss of her companion energy," Alana said, tenderly touching my arm. "And now, you feel the loss of me, as well."

Tears rolled down my cheeks as Alana's words pierced my heart, yet her eyes held me fast and I could not look away from her.

"I will never leave you. I could never leave you, daughter of Soul." Alana's voice was gentler than I had ever heard her speak. "You know that, don't you?"

"Yes." I knew it, but I also knew that her physical presence would no longer be available to me, except in memory, and the feeling of not being able to sit with her was more than I could bear.

"Read me what you wrote in your book about "Companion Energy," Alana said.

I hesitated, then wiped the tears from my face, and thumbed through my papers until I came to that section of the book.

COMPANION ENERGY

True love and sharing is divine, and being with one who is a companion in this way, produces an energy that is both healing and uplifting. When one person climbs a ladder to pick a peach from the limb of a tree, the other is there to make sure that the platform is steady. Likewise, when the other strikes out on a new adventure of the spirit, the first is there to cheer her on. One is always boosting the other, without interference or manipulation of any kind. The pure companion energy of true friends is kin to our Earth Mother, nurturing the seeds that fall into her soil. She does not tell them how to grow. Instead, she allows the natural forces of rain, sunshine, and wind to assist in the growth. Likewise, one who serves another in companion energy is served. The giver is the receiver, just as the soil is enriched by that which grows in it. Leaves fall to the ground to decompose, forming mulch which enriches the earth. In other words, give to life and life will give to you.

"Walking in companion energy means to be in agreement with the world around you. The world does not decide who you are and you do not decide what the world is. When there is an acceptance between the two, there is companion energy.

Woman Between the Wind
Page 91

"You make energy by shifting the existing energy."

Flight of Winged Wolf
Page 139

"Companion energy with anything is to accept where you are and who you are without highs or lows in feeling. To be one with the forest is to have no opinion about it one way or the other."

Woman Between the Wind
Page 93

"While we must learn to
stand alone, no one can truly
stand alone."

Circle of Power
Page 39

"We can be nourished by
something we do not like, but the
nourishment is of a lower order
and there is not then a companion
energy. The idea is not to like or
dislike anything, but instead to
live in acceptance of the energies
around us. It is acceptance of
an energy that makes it a
companion energy.

Woman Between the Wind
Page 112

"I became conscious of myself
with Alana and everything around
us at the same time.
I was perceiving energy rather
than grasping at feeling
and sensations."

Circle of Power
Page 9

"We are all channeling (directing)
energies to each other all the time.
The world is a sea of energy and
we are submerged in it."

Woman Between the Wind
Page 115

"If things happen to you it is
because you are attracted to the
things that happen to you.
It means that you are attracted to a
story within the sea of energy and
you are trying to live it. I am
only a vehicle for that which
attracts you."

Woman Between the Wind
Page 116

"A shaman is so adept at shape shifting that he or she can become like a river, or a drop of water, or a mountain lion, a wolf, or even an eagle."

Flight of Winged Wolf
Page 20

"Shape shifting is the very essence of communication. When we are trying to understand another person's idea or we try to get them to understand ours, we shape-shift with that individual; that is, we make the effort to match energies with them."

Flight of Winged Wolf
Page 61

"When you are working with companion energy, there is no resistance."

Flight of Winged Wolf
Page 86

"Strong energy draws strong reaction."

Flight of Winged Wolf
Page 50

"When you become accustomed to matching energies with all life, you will no longer fear anything."

Flight of Winged Wolf
Page 126

"When you have a consuming desire to do something you are being led by your emotions and not by your consciousness."

Flight of Winged Wolf
Page 66

PROCRASTINATION

The face of procrastination is one-sided and that in itself should be a striking revelation to anyone who indulges herself in wearing it. By one-sided I mean that there is no redeeming factor to procrastination. That which you want remains at a distance because you take less than necessary action to achieve it. In other words, procrastination is very inflexible, because it limits movement. Wearing such a face, makes one discontented and dissatisfied with life, so much so that the procrastinator often becomes very critical of himself, other people and the world at large. At best, the procrastinator keeps these opinions to himself, which often is released through the consumption of alcohol or other drugs. Sometimes an anti-depressant seems to be necessary for these people, because they hold so much anger inside of themselves. Yes, anger. Depression is anger turned inward, or negative feeling unexpressed. Some legal drugs seem to transmute this depression into a sense of well-being, only the comfort zone ceases to exist once the drug is discontinued, and the side effects of these drugs make it impossible for one to consume them forever. Procrastination is the germ of inertia. Inertia means movement without actions, in other words, the flow of life simply forces situations to change in a person's life. When, after a time, they have done nothing but procrastinate. As inertia settles into an individual's life, she becomes a victim, another person's victim, sociological, environmental victim. She becomes the victim of circumstances, whatever it may be.

So why procrastinate?

People usually procrastinate after they have lost their confidence to do something correctly. Perhaps they have a procrastinator in their family, who, in their fear for themselves, conveyed that fear to their offspring. Parental effects can be very dramatic on a child. "If one makes an effort they may fail," or "If one makes an effort and succeeds, new responsibilities will spring up which may cause failure. Then, when you lose everything, you'll have much to lose." It's like the person who worries that if she gets too successful she will have to pay high taxes.

Life does not need to be so complicated. People need only to make choices and to take action to make them come about. If one hesitates too long, she may miss a moment of fruition. But don't let that idea stop you either. Missing one's moment in time is not a valid reason for procrastination. Life operates in cycles. If you miss one timely moment, there will always be another.

"Schizophrenia occurs when an individual is in conflict between thoughts and emotions.
She thinks one thing and feels the opposite..."

Flight of Winged Wolf
Page 18

"The schizophrenic state is all-seeing, all-knowing with no DO."

Flight of Winged Wolf
Page 108

"Flexibility is when everything is okay as it is. When you accept change, you are being flexible. Trying to change everything around to have it the way you want it is being inflexible."

Woman Between the Wind
Page 58

"There is always junk sitting around somewhere. ...if you don't want it, don't pick it up. Pick up only the good stuff..."

Flight of Winged Wolf
Page 97

"Each of us can only be what we are. When we are anything else, we become inflexible."

Woman Between the Wind
Page 62

"When you can be willful and content at the same time, then your willfulness will work for you instead of against you."

Woman Between the Wind
Page 63

"When a person decides to do something, it is important for her to go all the way, but she must take responsibility for what she does. No matter what she does, she must first know why she is doing it, and then continue without doubt or remorse about it."

Woman Between the Wind
Page 82

"You could never quite push through the barriers in your life because you deluded yourself into believing that the barriers were your life."

Flight of Winged Wolf
Page 19

"Addiction is resistance to something and hanging onto it at the same time."

Flight of Winged Wolf
Page 53

Alana then asked me to talk about old age and having an elderly parent.

OLD AGE

Old age culminates youth and the middle years of one's life. In old age one lives the harvest of one's youth and middle years. Whatever you have put into life remains a part of you. This is not to say that you will have the same quantity or quality of your youth or middle years but that which you did will remain a part of you always. Happiness is gained by being mentally free. Most likely, if you were attached to worry and strife in your youth and middle years, your worry and strife will continue into old age, unless you are willing to put it down. However, if you were a person who always sought freedom for a better life, giving and sharing and loving, your later years should be filled with wisdom and joy. When you plant an orange seed, the outcome should be an orange tree. Old age should be like living as a mature orange tree. The quality of fruit produced is the result of the strength and health of the tree that bore it. Finally, when the tree is too old to bear fruit, it will be pruned and cut into fire wood. The stump and roots will be removed to make a way for sapling trees that are growing in its place. There is nothing sad about this process. It is the way it is, and life continues.

TO THE CHILDREN OF AGING PARENTS

Do not judge your parents. Instead, love them by accepting them for who they are. No doubt, they made plenty of mistakes in their lives and you may feel that some of those mistakes were against you. No matter. Try to remember the good times. In most cases, even in bad times, your parents had no intention of injuring you. The pain they felt turned into the pain you felt.

Parenting is something no one knows how to do until they do it. From mistakes, we learn what we could have done instead. Most mistakes were honest, loving ones. They were errors made in an effort to save the family and to protect you, their children and to guide you. So you see, it does no good to blame your parents when they did the best they could at the time they reared you. And, while you are into forgiving your parents, understand that you, too, as a parent, have made mistakes, perhaps not the same ones your parents made but then, your children will most likely not make the same mistakes that you made either.

So, honor your parents, by being the best you can be now, and by accepting them for being the best that they could be. Keep guilt out of your relationship and, instead, respect your parents for the efforts they made. Respect them, not necessarily in personality (which may be filled with traits you do not like) but, rather, respect them as Soul, of which you are a part.

PART 4

THE DELICATE SONG
OF GRASS GROWING

Alana straightened her sitting position, then leaned back against the wall of the cave again. "We should talk about the shanunpa of our lineage, and how it affects you through my leaving."

I nodded and looked away. While I respected her choice to leave, I felt traumatized by it as well. I knew that discussion of the shanunpa of our lineage was near the final step, before her departure from life.

Shanunpa (sha-nun-pa) referred to the song or language of persons or things. Alana had taught me that all things have language, and that to communicate with anything all you had to do was to recognize that language and imitate it. Communication referred to understanding the nature of a thing. For instance, to understand the river and to learn its mysteries, you had to be very still and listen to the sounds the river makes. If you sit quietly and long enough, the language the river uses will become distinguishable and you will be able to imitate it. Once you can do this, you can understand what it is saying and listen to the stories it has to tell. All things have stories. Trees tell their stories partially through their green leaves. The voice of the tree speaks through the green or by what science calls oxygen. Trees also produce a scent voice that speaks to butterflies and other insects who like to eat it. Sometimes the tree will emit an odor to repel a type of insect. This odor is the tree's way of communicating. If you are sensitive enough you can translate its language through your senses, just as the insects do. Shanunpa confirms that every creature and object has a song, and that the singing of a song is natures' lure to attract or repel its listener. The secret power of shanunpa is in learning to listen to the songs of life. It is a deeply spiritual practice that requires the instruction of a shaman teacher. It cannot be taught to an apprentice until she has come fully face-to-face with her own personal myth or story. The principle is that one must first recognize her own song before she can recognize the songs of life. All this process must occur prior to an apprentice becoming a Thunderbeing or "conscious" source of serviceable energy, the first great step to becoming shaman. The song of the shaman occurs when one is able to practice shanunpa with her teacher. This is a time when the merger between shaman and apprentice begins.

"Shanunpa is the way of our lineage," Alana added. "Without it there would be no lineage." I nodded that I understood. "You and I have experienced shanunpa on many, many levels," she continued. "And now it must occur on the final and greatest level of them all."

The cave suddenly became very bright, so bright that the features on Alana's face became indistinguishable. After a moment, the light dimmed and became as it had been. I knew there was not much time left and yet I could think of nothing to say. Mostly, I felt content and whole but it was bittersweet, and the contentment had a sting to it, as well.

"The silence between us exists because we share the forces of life. Your being and mine are living together," Alana said softly. Then she said something so quietly that I had to place my ear next to her lips to hear. What I heard were not really syllables but more like the delicate song of a field of growing wheat grass. Alana smiled sweetly at me. "Read me more of your book," she said.

MEDITATION

Meditation is good, and sitting in quiet repose for twenty minutes, or two hours out of every day will certainly enrich your life with a feeling of doing something for your spiritual growth. After you have meditated, you can go out into the world and say to yourself, where I have been and where I am are different from where I am going. This is the illusion of the meditator. In fact, there is no difference in where you have been, where you are, and where you are going, no difference at all. The three directions are merged in the present moment, this moment, NOW. But to the meditator this truth is a puzzle, remaining to be solved.

There is no puzzle. There is no solution. There is no more than what IS. When the meditator realizes that life itself is the meditation then the meditative state comes without difficulty or strain.

The reason so many find meditation a strain is that they have been taught one of two ways: 1) To hold thoughts at bay, which is a tedious task, or 2) to contemplate on an aspect of spiritual truth, or on the image of their teacher. I've already said that the first method is tedious. The second is like leaving a child unattended in a candy shop after telling him he can eat only one piece. Even if the child manages to obey, which is doubtful, he will not taste the piece of candy he chose to eat. Instead, he will be sensing all of the other flavors he has denied himself.

The only worthwhile meditation begins by practicing the attention at the Third Eye. Here, one becomes enlivened as Soul. It's a practice that can be accomplished while working at one's job, while grocery shopping, while going to the post office, while visiting with family or friends, or even hiking in the hills. This type of meditation enlivens not only the practitioner but everyone the practitioner meets. In this way, life becomes a meditation for you and everyone you touch throughout the day.

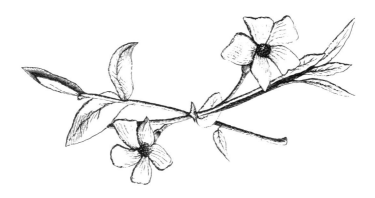

"It is wise to meditate in a group or alone with your eyes open. In this way you will stay in your body, aware of living in the present moment, and remain grounded to the earth. As you go along, you will notice that, as Soul, life is a living meditation and gradually you will no longer feel the "need" to meditate. When you are truly comfortable in this awareness, you will naturally explore the "here and now" of other dimensions.

Please do not rush this. If you follow the instructions I give you, your life will be centered and exceedingly fruitful. Most people who rush into out-of-body experiences without proper preparation find their outer life in mounting chaos."

– from a letter to an apprentice

CONTEMPLATION

Contemplation is visualization of a spiritual principle or of the image of a spiritual adept. Some people also use this as a means of creative visualization, to bring to themselves persons or material objects. It's all the same, really. Since most people contemplate in order to bring that which is lacking into their lives - be it spiritual principle, teacher or material objects - the result is to try to fill some hole, some emptiness. Have you ever tried to fill a main line gopher hole with water? There seems to be no end to it. The hose can run water full force for hours into the hole and still never fill it. This is because the emptiness is vast, spreading out over an entire field.

If you want to fill yourself with spiritual principles, focus your attention at the Third Eye. The desire for perfection will be immediately cut off and, in the place of desire, will be a recognition of the spirituality of all life. The same is true for those seeking material objects. Since you already carry the seeds of everything you need and want inside of yourself, when you cease trying to conjure through creative visualization, trying to manipulate energies, that which you require or want will automatically come marching toward you. Why is this so? When one tries to bring something to herself through visualization, she unwittingly omits pieces of the image desired. Thus, she either receives an incomplete image of her desire or unknowingly pushes the image away through conflicting efforts. You see, the only type of effort that is valuable results from the effortless effort produced from living as Soul.

MANTRAS

Mantras can sometimes be useful to quiet a greatly agitated mind. By repeating a word or phrase over and over again, silently or aloud, the mind becomes mesmerized and a state of self-hypnosis sets in. In using this method, as soon as the mind is quiet, the aspirant should fasten his/her attention onto the Third Eye, the seat of Soul, where the mind can move into usefulness again without becoming agitated.

The use of mantras should be limited to emergencies only, when one is not able to otherwise shift her attention to the Third Eye center. The reason mantras should be used in such a limited manner is that mantras tend to make the mind exceedingly dull, almost stupid. Living from the Third Eye produces mental brilliance because the mind is enlivened by Soul to express its nature within the environment.

SOUL RETRIEVAL

We are hearing much about this subject these days. Some of it is responsible, and some of it is irresponsible. A responsible practice of Soul Retrieval, and its true meaning, is to reclaim energy from stuck places in our lives, from childhood, adolescence, and adulthood right up to the present moment. This is accomplished through a specific repetitive exercise, practiced alone, which my apprentices experience in their 8th Journey, titled "Reclaiming Your Energy." Don Juan referred to this as "recapitulation," in the Casteneda related books. While each teacher calls it by a different name, the practice is the same and it is ALWAYS accomplished alone.

The irresponsible method, which is directed by a group leader for an exorbitant fee, often produces undesirable effects. Instead of reclaiming a person's energy from the past and empowering her in the present, there is a shift of past-stuck energy into a present moment mental crutch. Mental crutches are mental inventions, energy that is allowed to chatter away inside the skull, convincing the participant of the presence of a higher being guiding her actions. It does not take long, however, before the so-called inner

guidance received proves faulty. The long-ago problems that were brought to the surface by improper
methods begin to direct one's life in a disastrous way.
I suggest, if you feel you must investigate popular
systems of Soul Retrieval, that you keep your eyes
open. I mean for you to literally keep them open while
you are performing the exercise the leader gives you.
In that way you will maintain a "ground" to your
solar center.

"Energy often does come from outside an individual.
A conscious person knows how to draw energy from the forces around her; an unconscious person is a victim of it. It is not my theory that body language channels (directs) energy, but shaman knowledge."

Woman Between the Wind
Page 106

DIVINATION

There are times in life when it is difficult to see ahead and these are times when you may find yourself seeking information about the future. This is natural. It is oftentimes easier to see the future of a friend or family member than it is your own. If you feel the need of looking into a future situation, however, don't ask someone else to tell you what they see. In other words, don't go for a clairvoyant "reading." These readings are tainted, and often distorted by the reader's state of consciousness. Instead use your own faculties to discover what you need to know. There are many tools out there in the marketplace to assist you. I Ching, Runes, Medicine and Tarot cards can all assist you to look into yourself. When you use these, first shift your attention to the Third Eye, which will direct your consciousness to the seat of Soul. You can then accept what is given you.

An even better method of divination is to shift your attention to the Third Eye, seat of Soul, and then go out into the world to see what striking occurrences are presented to you. Observe without mental comment. Simply look at what you see happening in the environment. If your body reacts with some sort of feeling, pay attention to it, without analyzing what you feel. The feeling may trigger emotions, which you should quickly dismiss. If emotions are triggered, it means your attention is no longer centered on the Third Eye. Emotions are not the type of feeling we are referring to. Life itself is a feeling, acknowledged by our body senses at the moment we lock our higher attention on to something. It can be something as simple as a cat running across the street or something as dramatic as a low flying plane. Was a feeling conveyed to you by that which was presented? This may take some practice but the effort is worthwhile. In this way, life itself becomes your method of divination, which is really part of the service that life provides. Give it a try. When you return to your home, which is your medicine lodge, write down what you encountered in your journal.

The light in the cave dimmed. I paused and looked at Alana. She lifted her hand to reassure me that she was all right. "I have written about the shanunpa of perceiving the invisible world," I said, wanting to peek her interest. She opened her eyes and gazed at me. The light in the cave suddenly brightened. I turned the page of my book. The next subject was the shununpa of the invisible, or clairvoyance.

CLAIRVOYANCE/CLAIRAUDIENCE

Clairvoyance means to perceive what is not visibly present, whereas clairaudience means to hear what is taking place within the silence. This is accomplished by tuning in to the energy of someone, something or some environment and recognizing what is there without actually seeing it with your eyes or hearing it with your ears. It is relative to intuition except that intuition is personal and clairvoyance/ clairaudience is usually not personal. In its purest form, clairvoyance/clairaudience is an art and often they live together.

The purest form of these arts is a manner of detached perception, wherein the perceiver's attitudes and opinions are removed from that which is being perceived. In other words, true clairvoyance is Soul Vision or sight that stems from the Third Eye at the center of one's forehead. When an individual becomes adept at living from that seat of Soul, clairvoyance and clairaudience naturally come into play in a person's life. What happens then is truly wonderful!

The waves of movement, or voice of elemental energy, touches a subject at a transitional time, or encourages it to move at the precise moment when transition can occur and the person, who is living as Soul, witnesses the change in appearance and sound. Within the capsule of the moment, they know its past, its present and its future.

The more one lives as Soul, the more clairvoyant one becomes. Whatever they look at speaks to them (shanunpa). Soul uses the psychic forces just as Soul uses the mind and its intellect. The difference between this approach to clairvoyance/clairaudience and that which is commonly described, is that all stems from Soul or the God-Self of the individual, rather than the mind and its emotions trying to tap into Soul.

"It is the clairvoyant in a person that can be extremely dangerous. When this faculty is developed in a person, they have a special power to manipulate and control the minds of others. When you least expect it they may be taking you over (by intermingling their attitudes and opinions)."

Circle of Power
Page 10

"You need to have your strings of energy tied down in order to move forward spiritually."

Circle of Power
Page 20

Alana opened her eyes and then closed them, and once again the light in the cave dimmed. "I am not finished," I said, not wanting her to leave. I quickly continued reading.

CHANNELING

This is a very touchy subject, so I will begin by saying that the nature of my comments is not to pass judgment on "channeling," but to present the facts about what "channeling" is and isn't, so that you can intelligently decide for yourself.

The word "channel" in this instance means "conduit" or "passageway" through which energies from another dimension can flow. Since we, Soul, live in the physical plane in physical bodies, energies from another dimension must use a physical vehicle to be able to express itself in the physical world.

The entities that use physical channels are inorganic beings or physically invisible energy masses that contain knowledge of the universes and the modus operandi of all life. The reason that they contain this wondrous knowledge is that they are a part of it, but on a dimensional level just beneath the one in which we live. These inorganic beings have never incarnated, except as an expression that is accepted by a human who is willing to share their physical vehicle or body with them. The consciousness of these beings is an

120

impulse which drives itself toward physical expression. The driving impulse the inorganic beings possess is without conscience. It doesn't care about the well-being of the occupant it shares a body with because it will eagerly dominate or take possession of a body if given the opportunity. First, it must lure the present occupant and convince the individual of the opportunities it has to offer through co-existence. These include divine knowledge and a promise to eliminate loneliness. What it doesn't tell is that the original occupant will maintain the body less and less and, as this process occurs, the outer life disintegrates even though the inner life of the person may seem rich and rewarding. Families break up for no apparent reason. The individual loses his job, has difficulty relating to friends, neighbors and the environment at large. Very often the host occupant will display obsessive and/or addictive behavior that is totally out of character. He or she will often lose all of their material possessions and their health. In other words, being a channel for an inorganic energy sets one up for a transference of energy to occupy the body. This transference can be sudden or it can take months or even years to complete. In other writings, you have heard this spoken of as a "walk in."

FLYING SAUCERS

They exist. There is life on other planets in our universe, and in other universes. Some of these life forms are elevated in consciousness, higher than human, and some are lower in consciousness. Those higher in consciousness know that to interfere with the progress of human life, to direct it or influence it in any way, is a violation of universal law. Those lower in consciousness have a desire to participate, and actively search for opportunities to do so - to guide and coach, to regulate and command the movement of life on our planet.

One apprentice wrote me that he had a re-occurring dream of some space people asking for his help in healing a disease one of their people had contacted while visiting earth. They told him that the disease had now become a plague on their planet. Since he was not a physician, he asked what they wanted him to do but they never answered him. The dream was so intense, real-like, that it haunted the dreamer for years. I told him that I felt these aliens were ingesting his energy, feeding on it by tuning in to his ego by saying that they needed his help, which in turn engaged his attention. If one's attention is fastened on something, an invisible string of energy connects the subject and the object. The only way to free that energy, reclaim or retrieve it, is to shift the attention to the safety zone in a person's body, the seat of Soul in the center of the forehead, called the Tisra Til or Third Eye. In this way, the host parasite also develops its own strength as Soul, and no longer requires to sap energy from another.

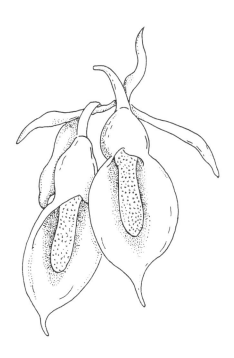

SPIRIT GUIDES

Anyone we remember, even after their death, is still connected to us. The degree of the connection corresponds to the degree of the memory. If you feel them intensely, they are very close, otherwise you would sense their presence at a distance. If, for any reason, you want them close, to assist in some way, and they seem very far away, simply imagine them and yearn to be close to them. Wherever they are, they respond to the tug of the string of energy connecting you.

There is another kind of spirit guide, the personality of someone you knew (or were) in a past life, who is still residing in the worlds of imaginary vision, which is the astral plane. For some reason connected to unfinished business, a personality can reside in the astral plane, which looks very much like Earth, only more refined in vibration (color, space, sensation, etc.) for thousands of years. You may die and be incarnated dozens of times to their one, and, for those dozens of times that you returned, they will continue to respond to the string of energy between you, often called a karmic bond.

PSYCHIC SELF-PROTECTION

When you are afraid of someone, you give them power over you, so don't be afraid, no matter how fierce they may seem. You can respect someone without fearing them and if you cannot shake the fear that your respect brings, there is something wrong. You are going to have to take a long, hard look at yourself to see what it is that attracts you to the one you fear. Yes, attract. If you were not attracted to them, you would not pay them so much attention. Let go. I used to complain to my teacher Alana Spirit Changer about certain things and people, and how I felt trapped by them. She'd say to me, "If you don't like what you see or it makes you uncomfortable, why do you look at it?" At other times, I'd tell her about somebody's attitude or about something that was happening in the world that really upset me. Alana would shake her head. "You collect garbage wherever you go," she said. "Empty your hands. Let go of what you hear and see, and simply do not pick up garbage anymore." Another time I mentioned that I felt she and I were bound together forever and that the idea worried me. At this Alana laughed. "If you will let go of me we won't be so attached," she said. "I'm not holding onto you. You are holding onto me."

So you see, that which frightens us is that which we do not want in our lives, yet we hold it to us by our fear. Fear forms attraction, the stickiest kind of attraction. That which you desperately do not want is glued to you.

If you don't know how to stop fearing so much, listen to the signals your body sends you. When you feel your muscles tightening to form even the slightest resistance, drop your arms at your sides. Say, "Release!" preferably aloud. Then shift your attention to the Third Eye. If you are unable to sustain your attention there, drop your arms at your sides again. "Release!" Again, shift your attention to the Third Eye. If you need to do this many times in a day, it is okay. In this way, you will develop your attention at the seat of Soul, which means you are using your fear to empower you.

"When someone's difficulties in life leave you emotionally drained, it usually means you are staring at yourself through them. In everyday language, this condition is called sympathy. One who lives as Soul spends very little time staring into the mirror of self-reflection. Instead, she meets another's sorrow with "compassion," which is Soul's manner of feeling, a kind of feeling but not feeling, akin to divine love, or unconditional love. It can't really be called detachment because one who is detached often feels isolated. An isolated individual is staring at herself."

–from a letter to an apprentice

"You'll be happy to know that Soul is eternal and not subject to psychic attacks. However, the mind can suffer greatly from them. The ego, as you know, is easily bruised and, unfortunately, people psychically harm each other, sometimes to the point of death. Your realization of this power and your willingness to accept responsibility for your thoughts and actions, says that you are an evolving Soul."

–from a letter to an apprentice

"'Liking' and 'disliking' are merely flip sides of a coin, which is why neither really matters. Of course, we choose from one to the other, but we don't have to have rigid ideas on anything, meaning we can change to suit the moment."

–from a letter to an apprentice

PSYCHIC INTRUSION

If you feel someone is intruding in your psychic space, implanting thoughts and feelings in your mind, follow the advice given above. Use your challenge to empower you by keeping your attention on the Third Eye. And listen closely. Nothing can harm you as long as you are on your own path. This statement does not mean the Shaman path, the Buddha path or the Christian path. It means the path of you as Soul. With your attention on the Third Eye, you are living as Soul and nothing can harm you. If someone is trying to intrude in your thoughts, shift your attention to the Third Eye and you will recognize the culprit and his motives, which removes you from the position of victim. Soul is never a victim, however the mind can be if it is allowed to run rampant, and not operated by Soul.

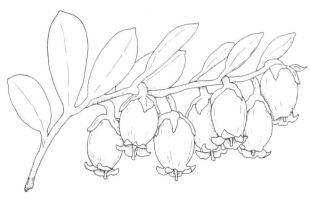

"I know there are some who practice witchcraft and call themselves shaman. They are not shaman. A witch mani–pulates the forces of nature and the energies of others. A shaman never manipulates. There is no reason to do so. A shaman lives as Soul in a physical body. Whatever is needed is provided. There is no reason to manipulate to gain power. Once you learn to live as Soul, the energy of life fills you. My intent in training you is to remove the barriers that keep you from living in your power, or as Soul. Power, to me, is joy, a result of being a living expression of unconditional love."

–from a letter to an apprentice

"Fear is a disease spread primarily by religions and people acting on behalf of them. Never forget that, and you will never let fear stand in your way. What you fear cannot harm you - but the fear itself has great power. As you move along in your apprenticeship, your fears will leave you, although the old feelings may rear their heads for awhile. Your apprenticeship is to empower you to freedom, where fear does not exist. This freedom comes from living as Soul."

–from a letter to an apprentice

"If you are being controlled by someone or something, it is because you won't let go of him or it."

Flight of Winged Wolf
Page 97

"Conflict is mental entrapment, usually born out of fear - "But what if this...but what if that..?" Soul never fears. It exists independently of any mental conflict. Neither is guilt a part of Soul's existence. Soul is all-powerful, omnipresent, omniscient and omnipotent. Mastership = living as Soul, which means to be free of domination of persons, religions, things, and/or mental traps. We are all Soul, and, being Soul - ONE - no one is better than another."

–from a letter to an apprentice

"Stuck energy is usually fear energy. This occurs when we know that moving forward necessitates change. Change is an unknown, at least mentally... I encourage you with, "It's okay!" The only thing you have to fear is fear, and I understand what it is you are fearing. There is no freedom in fear. Fear constricts."

–from a letter to an apprentice

"No need to try to change a belief systems because it would then only become another belief system - and all have limitations. Simply learn to look at beliefs, acknowledge them for what they are, and don't give them more importance than that. The rule applies to the presence of fear. If you look at fear without mulling it over, which causes it to escalate, it cannot control your life."

–from a letter to an apprentice

"Any difficulties you may perceive in the environment, including psychic disturbances, can be used as an X (trigger) to get you in to Soul Vision. In this way, disturbances will no long bother you. Instead, they will empower you, because you will use them as a reminder to live as Soul."

–from a letter to an apprentice

EMPOWERMENT

Empowerment is the DO of enlightenment or, in other words, it is the wisdom of enlightenment put to work in one's life. My beloved teacher Alana Spirit Changer always told me that "knowledge learned off of the path was useless" and that people would be better off, knowing only that which they could live. She explained that having an abundance of knowledge that could not be lived, actually encumbers a person by giving her an illusionary sense of empowerment. (In fact, it usually makes them schizophrenic.) Enlightenment has to be enlivened with action to be EMPOWERMENT and, when these two actions occur - ENLIGHTENMENT + ACTION - everything about a person's life improves. Of course, the action that walks with enlightenment, while seemingly ordinary, is no ordinary action. Every movement is precisely aligned to walk in step with the perception, knowledge and wisdom of the enlightened individual. Therefore, the results are freedom, joy, giving, receiving and further abundance on all levels.

"You are here in this physical life to learn to live as Soul in a physical body. Soul Vision is about living as power. With your attention on the third eye, in the center of your forehead, you are living as Soul, using the physical body as a vehicle."

Circle of Power
Page 98

"Living from this Soul viewpoint you will discover a life of bliss and unqualified abundance."

Circle of Power
Page 98

"Life is precious, which is why it was given to us. Here, living in a physical body, on the earth, Soul becomes empowered to Be Itself and to realize God, which It does when It realizes Itself to be a part of God. But these are merely words until the day comes when you wear them as an Awakened Consciousness."

Circle of Power
Page 98

"To achieve power, one must let go and surrender."

Circle of Power
Page 40

"Everything is already created, so there is nothing to create. You present a thing into being through your attention and feeling."

Circle of Power
Page 43

"To present something into existence then would be to feel it into the present moment."

Circle of Power
Page 51

"...the real wonder and magic of life occurs NOW, in the exact instant it is lived. Thought and feeling had to be aligned with the present instant, or miss the point."

Circle of Power
Page 87

"Alana!"

Alana opened her eyes and looked at me. "You have finished your book," she said.

"Yes."

"I love you, my daughter," she said sweetly.

"I love you, my mother," I answered.

"Where is your eagle stick?" Alana asked.

I reached behind me and held it up for her to see. She raised her hand and touched the face of the eagle, then began to whisper something. I put my cheek to her lips. "I am not dying," Alana said faintly, "I am living!"

I could say nothing and I dared not move. I stayed bent over her for a long time. The events of my years of apprenticeship with her passed in front of my eyes, and I knew what she said was true. The subject of her translation was life, not death, and that as Soul, we were ONE.

Gradually, I raised up and opened my eyes. The cave was brilliant, completely flooded with an intense, nearly blinding light. I held the eagle stick to my heart and reached to touch my teacher with my other hand but, instead of touching Alana, I touched the rug where she had lain. Alana's body was no longer there. I remained motionless for a long time and then, finally, I rose to my feet. The light moved with me, enfolding me, and remained with me as I returned to my life and my work.

ORDER FORM / 800-336-6015

Please send me the following:

Quantity	Book Title or Item	Price	Amt.
_____	THE SHAMANIC JOURNEY OF LIVING AS SOUL	10.00	_____
_____	CIRCLE OF POWER	10.00	_____
_____	THE FLIGHT OF WINGED WOLF	10.00	_____
_____	WOMAN BETWEEN THE WIND	10.00	_____
_____	THE SHAMAN OF TIBET	14.95	_____
_____	WRITING AS A TOOL FOR SELF-DISCOVERY	9.95	_____
_____	DOORWAYS BETWEEN THE WORLDS	9.95	_____

CASSETTE TAPES

Quantity	Item	Price	Amt.
_____	SAN FRANCISCO LECTURE	9.95	_____
_____	LIVING AS SOUL	9.95	_____
_____	POWER OF SPOKEN WORD/CONSCIOUSNESS	9.95	_____
_____	ABUNDANCE	9.95	_____

SHIPPING: $3.00 one item, $1.00 each additional item.   _____

☐ I WANT TO BECOME A MEMBER OF THE EAGLE TRIBE. ENCLOSED IS MY ANNUAL MEMBERSHIP FEE OF $25.00

☐ PLEASE SEND ME AN APPLICATION FOR APPRENTICESHIP.

TOTAL (USA funds only) $ _____

PHONE ORDERS: 800-336-6015

Please print:

NAME: _____ PHONE:(_____)_____

ADDRESS: _____

CITY, STATE, ZIP: _____

VISA/MASTERCARD NUMBER: _____

EXP DATE: _____ SIGNATURE: _____

ALSO AVAILABLE AT YOUR BOOKSTORE

Higher Consciousness Books
Post Office Box 1797 • Cottonwood, AZ 86326 • Phone/FAX (602) 634-7728

AN INVITATION
Become a Member of The Eagle Tribe

The Eagle Tribe, founded in 1992, is a flock of high-spirited individuals who have joined together for personal enjoyment and spiritual expansion within a society for higher consciousness/shamanic study and exploration. These individuals come from every walk of life and every profession to enjoy a lofty camaraderie that has no dogma or creed to bind them.

The Eagle Tribe erases racial boundaries. It is not American Indian, although it does honor nature and natural law, the tradition in which I was taught. As you will recall in my book, **Woman Between the Wind**, Alana Spirit Changer stressed the importance of non-Native Americans not trying to live the American Indian life. She stressed that "the teachings live by themselves" (have a life of their own), so that non-Native Americans could easily adapt it to life in their own culture.

All apprentices are Eagle Tribe members, but NOT all members are apprentices, nor is it important for them to be so. There is an expression that "Water seeks its own level," which means that individuals with similar direction in life will come together to learn and to mutually enjoy activities and togetherness. Our newsletter (which will eventually grow into a magazine), **The Eagle's Cry**, will keep people posted about the Tribe's growth and activity. The number of activities will expand and grow as the Tribe grows. In the spirit of ONE-NESS, it is also the intent of **The Eagle Tribe** to attract participation from other medicine people and/or shaman from other tribes, in addition to accomplished people in every field of endeavor.

Your participation is welcome. Dues are $25.00 a year. I look forward to meeting many of you throughout the year.

Enjoy balance with the earth. Walk with soft-eyed vision.

—*Winged Wolf*

Higher Consciousness Books
P. O. Box 1797
Cottonwood, AZ 86326

Higher Consciousness Books
P. O. Box 1797
Cottonwood, AZ 86326

If you wish to receive a copy of the latest catalog/newsletter and be placed on our mailing list, please send us this card.

Please print

Name: _____

Address: _____

City & State: _____

Zip: _____ Country: _____

- -

If you wish to receive a copy of the latest catalog/newsletter and be placed on our mailing list, please send us this card.

Please print

Name: _____

Address: _____

City & State: _____

Zip: _____ Country: _____